PERILS
OF
PARADISE

Rita Beamish

3565 Harding Ave.
Honolulu, Hawai'i 96816
Phone: (800) 910-2377
Fax: (808) 732-3627
www.besspress.com

Design: Carol Colbath

All photos by author, except where indicated.

Library of Congress Cataloging-in-Publication Data

Beamish, Rita.
  Perils of paradise / Rita
Beamish.
     p. cm.
  Includes illustrations, bibliography.
  ISBN 1-57306-168-9
  1. Accidents - Hawaii - Anecdotes.
  2. Natural disasters - Hawaii –
Anecdotes. 3. Hawaii - Miscellanea.
  I. Title.
  DU623.25.B43 2004   996-dc21

Printed in Korea

Contents

Acknowledgments

The stories in this book could only be told with the generous cooperation of the people who lived them. Their fortitude when facing the perils of paradise is a testament to human endurance and inspiration. My sincere thanks go to those who survived to tell their tales, as well as those who risked themselves in the rescues and then graciously shared the details with me: Hugh Alexander, Michael Coots, Craig Davidson, Scott Gordon, Keith Karasic, Larry Katahira, Brian Keaulana, Ernie Kosaka, Gene Kridler, Kyle Maligro, Marsue McShane, Leo Ohai, Peter Paton, Jonathan Stockton, Jack Straka, and Timothy Twigg-Smith. My thanks also to those who provided additional firsthand detail and background information for these stories: Justin Acosta, Michael Cowan, Beverly Creamer, John Cross, Walter Dudley, Ralph Goto, Lissa Guild, Steven Hedlund, Jim Jacobi, Jack Jeffrey, Norrie Judd, Lilikala Kameʻeleihiwa, Mardie Lane, Laurie MacIvor, Mark Marshall, Barbara Maxfield, John Naughton, Levon Ohai, Nephi Ohai, Gary Phillips, Kenneth Rubin, Erica Ryan, J. Michael Scott, and Jill Sommer. Finally, I could not have completed this book without the endless support and patience of my husband Paul Costello and my daughters Kelly and Kira.

Introduction

It's happened to many of us—islanders who revel in Hawai'i's outdoor life, and the millions who visit Hawai'i each year for a taste of paradise. An unexpected storm, a slippery hiking trail, an ocean current that turns aggressive. Caught without a cellular phone, a companion, the right footgear, or safety flares, we get lost or banged up a bit. But we live through it, maybe with a story that can be enlarged in the telling. Perhaps no preparation could have prevented the mishap, but the outcome certainly could have been more serious. So the experience inevitably prompts a mental note to be more cautious the next time. Just as inevitably, those mental notes recede. It's easy to be lulled again by the islands' lush and gentle ambience, because Hawai'i, in the end, is simply a place where danger seems remote.

The reality is that Hawai'i does have another side, a whole inventory of natural forces that demand respect and understanding. This reality was well known to the early Hawaiians, whose tradition was steeped in the interrelationships among all living things. Their deities embodied the bounty of the land, air, and water, and life was explained by the presence of supernatural beings and ancestors in the forces of nature as well as in everyday needs like crops, fish, and healing plants. The Hawaiians also recognized what later inhabitants too often would overlook—that this pacific and nurturing environment also is a place of great power and peril. Hawaiian legends and culture tell of gods who could launch disaster as well as beneficence, often in reaction to human failings or an imbalance in the natural order of things. The goddess Pele might trigger volcanic eruptions that erased entire villages. Mighty waves destroyed rock walls that protected fishponds. Tsunamis and hurricanes turned lives upside down, wiping out taro fields, crumpling homes, and claiming victims like so many overdue debts.

Such major disasters are infrequent, but there is no way, even today, of predicting when a near-shore earthquake will drown the coast in a tsunami or when a simmering volcano will send fiery lava to wipe out a forest. And even on a less dramatic scale, the suddenness with which Hawai'i can slip its benign façade and assert its power is a fact of life in the islands.

In a state with seven million visitors arriving each year, and a resident population of more than a million, the good news is that people don't find themselves on the losing side of this power more often. The same forces that give Hawai'i its unique appeal are also potential traps for those who take them lightly or who, like the people in this book, find themselves on the wrong side of nature more by happenstance than as a result of any misstep of their own. The people whose stories are told here learned that Hawai'i's rebukes are not reserved for daredevils and thrill seekers alone. Sometimes the misstep can be as ordinary as simply going to work one day—as did bird surveyor Peter Paton, doing the job for which he was so well trained; or Marsue McGinnis, teaching school on an exotic island; or Leo Ohai, piloting his plane on a routine fish-scouting flight; or Gene Kridler, for whom a little drama and adventure had become a well-rehearsed part of the job. Sometimes the victim is a visitor, like attorney Hugh Alexander, enjoying the paradise vacation he had dreamed about. Or a weekend adventurer, like teenager Timothy Twigg-Smith or hiker Jack Straka, neither of whom had reason to fear that his exploration of well-traveled backcountry would be anything other than rigorous and fun. Like kayaker Jon Stockton, they planned a mini-adventure, but nothing that appeared life-threatening, or even dangerous. Hawai'i had surprises on tap for all of them.

In terms of pure geography, Hawai'i's location in the middle of the Pacific Ocean is double-edged. The islands themselves are the product of volcanic eruptions over millions of years, with the youngest and easternmost, the Big Island of Hawai'i, still bubbling with active volcanoes. The curious can visit its molten lava flows, but multiple dangers await any who are incautious. And aside from the long, gradual slopes of those Big Island volcanoes, Hawai'i also boasts steep-sided, forested mountains with cliff trails that tower above crashing waves—trails that make for inviting hikes but also treacherous footing.

Additionally, Hawai'i's remoteness accounts for its abundant and unique plant and animal species, but this same isolation also renders the archipelago vulnerable to tsunami waves generated by faraway earthquakes, waves that race across the ocean unimpeded by any other land mass and bump into Hawai'i with full force. Similarly, while the balmy ocean makes Hawai'i a water sports paradise, those same waters are a key ingredient for hurricanes swooping in from the tropics. Most hurricanes spend themselves on the open sea before making landfall, but the ocean itself can turn angry at any time and unleash pounding surf to take out beaches or even roadways.

Although its history is studded with dramatic natural disasters, Hawai'i most often manifests its volatility in more mundane ways—with a sudden, localized rainstorm that floods a sunny day, or a nasty underwater current that claims a swimmer.

This book is about people in both situations: those who faced catastrophic events, and others who met peril in everyday situations. Their stories are not unlike those regularly reported in Hawai'i's newspapers, tales that are almost like background noise in the island state: The current grabs a snorkeler at Hanauma Bay. A tourist is swept away while viewing a waterfall. A teenager loses his life to O'ahu's famous Blowhole, which spews him into the air, then mercilessly slaps him onto the unforgiving rock. Hikers get stuck on a ledge, and a helicopter comes to their rescue. A surfer is pinned under tons of water, lucky that his lungs hold out, and survives with a broken limb. Two retirees set sail for California, then send a mayday call, the last anyone ever hears from them. Eight hikers die under a tragic rockfall that cascades onto the Sacred Falls trail.

Over the years, Hawai'i has kept the secrets of many others. On Kaua'i an enduring mystery surrounds a young couple from Massachusetts who walked into the Alaka'i Swamp one bright day and never came out. A mystery that has reached near-legend status surrounds the fate of Eddie Aikau, a renowned waterman, surfing champion, and heroic lifeguard who joined the native Hawaiian crew of a famous traditional sailing canoe in 1978. The *Hōkūle'a*, constructed in the traditional Polynesian style and piloted without modern navigational tools, was capsized by a storm, and Aikau heroically volunteered to paddle his surfboard for help. He disappeared into the whitecaps, pointing his board across the stormy ocean toward the nearest landfall twenty miles away. Although a rescue plane found the canoe and its crew, Aikau never was seen again.

Yet for every life claimed by Hawai'i's natural forces, many other would-be victims have survived, shrugged their shoulders, and headed back out to once again embrace the island environment. Sometimes the world hears all about these survivors—for instance, the thirteen-year-old, flaxen-haired surf champion Bethany Hamilton, who lost her arm to a shark in the fall of 2003 and with a resilience that won international attention soon returned to the waves, the essence of a positive outlook. This book recounts the strikingly similar shark story of bodyboarder Mike Coots, but the stories told here are not all from the same mold, nor did they all receive much media attention. These survivors met different perils with varied skills and survival knowledge, their challenges ranging from staying afloat in a stormy sea to just hanging on at the bottom of an earth crack. What they shared is an elusive quality, an ability to prevail against these overwhelming forces, aided by skill, luck, or an unseen power. They managed to overcome nature's toughest challenges, their triumph revealing an inner grit, and sometimes it was will alone that pulled them through in unexpected ways. These stories also highlight the spirit and bravery of rescuers who boldly risked themselves for strangers in trouble, pitting their training and skill against the same perilous conditions. All of the people depicted in the following pages have met Hawai'i's peril, and persevered and endured.

A Perfect Place

"I've got to get a picture of this!"

It wasn't fear-inspiring in the way that Marsue McGinnis had assumed a tidal wave would be, but it was unusual enough to photograph. On this first day of April, 1946, April Fool's Day, the ocean indeed was behaving oddly: sucking itself way back from the shore to reveal a sea bottom of flopping fish and seaweed and coral, then surging back to dump debris and sea life high above the normal shoreline. It was one of the stranger things that Marsue, a twenty-one-year-old schoolteacher, had seen. Only recently arrived in Hawai'i from Ohio, she was fascinated by the spectacle.

Marsue grabbed the little Leica camera that her grandfather had given her back home. She and Fay Johnson, her housemate and fellow teacher, stood on the porch of their seaside cottage. The ocean looked normal enough, its turquoise waters capped with frothy white surf, except that the waves were getting successively bigger, with that strange sucking action. Marsue raised her camera. She watched the ocean drain itself ominously across a vast, creepy expanse. Then a rushing wall of water quickly filled her lens. With a suddenness that thrust a stab of reality into her postcard photo frame, she knew the truth: it was coming for her. Fay saw it too, the awful peril jolting the two women simultaneously. For an eternal millisecond Marsue was paralyzed with horror. Then, "Let's go!"

Marsue dropped the camera and the two women lurched through the door, slamming it behind them. They raced the few paces across the living room toward the kitchen at the back of the cottage. From there they could escape to the adjacent sports field and run to higher ground. Their two housemates, Helen Kingseed and Dorothy Drake, came flying out of their bedrooms. At the kitchen door, the four women hesitated, not in panic but in unspoken confusion about whether bolting the cottage would be the safest course. A roar filled their ears. They grabbed the sides of the doorway. Marsue glanced back and saw the wave, now angry, blasting over the porch where she had just stood, its brown swirling waters clambering at the windows. The glass gave way as if it were paper. The walls groaned and the wave was upon them in a surge of power and fury. Marsue was shoved and lifted from her feet, then driven down into a watery brew of furnishings and friends. The cottage walls collapsed. The roof crashed down, then whirled, floating free like a crazy upside-down boat.

◇◇◇

It had seemed like a wonderful idea to the young woman just finishing her studies at Miami University in Oxford, Ohio. Teachers were needed in Hawai'i. In fact, "desperately" needed, according to the note that caught Marsue's attention on a campus bulletin board. She immediately perked up. The very notion was exciting, an exotic change from the wartime dreariness that had consumed her college years. She lived at home and had her horses and her studies, but there were no opportunities to travel, none of the summer trips abroad that an adventurous young woman like Marsue might have enjoyed in peacetime. On the social front, there were few men around, just a few fellows on campus who were deemed physically unfit for the military.

Exasperated with her sheltered life, the newly minted teacher jumped at the opportunity now before her. She finished her degree, then traveled by train to San Francisco. By now, the city was charged with the excitement of a newly arrived peace. President Truman had dropped the atomic bomb on Japan just a week earlier, and World War II at last was ended. Marsue boarded a Honolulu-bound sailing ship, the SS *Matsonia*. It was brimming with military officers and Seabees still on Pacific orders issued before Japan's surrender, and civilians returning home to Hawai'i after waiting out the war on the mainland.

The five-day journey deposited the passengers at Honolulu Harbor, gateway to a paradise Marsue had only dreamed about. There was a verve about the place. The territorial islands were emerging jubilant from the wartime curfews, blackouts, and bureaucracy they had endured under martial law, as they now began to ramp down the massive military apparatus that had fought the Pacific war.

For Marsue, the islands brought another new experience: her first air travel. It was 214 miles from Honolulu, which was located on the island of O'ahu, to the island of Hawai'i, called the Big Island, where she had been assigned to teach. Enroute, she looked from her airplane window down on the sleepy Hawaiian archipelago that had been born of successive volcanic eruptions millions of years earlier. Beyond Honolulu, the islands were rural, centered mostly on sugar and pineapple plantations. From the air, each island seemed to poke up like an oversized pebble from the sparkling ocean: slender Molokaʻi with its Kalaupapa Peninsula, a quarantine for leprosy patients; pastoral Maui with historic Kahoʻolawe on its flank; petite, lush Lānaʻi; and finally, the sprawling Big Island, where Marsue would teach in a plantation hamlet with the exotic-sounding name of Laupāhoehoe. The Big Island's geography flowed from five volcanoes whose sloping mountains now dominated the landscape, with multiple rivers of black, hardened lava extending from their summits to the ocean.

Landing at the busy town of Hilo, Marsue joined other teachers who also had answered the education department's call. The group piled into cars that met their plane, then motored across the island, stopping to drop off teachers at successive plantation schools. Several miles north of Hilo, Marsue's car turned from the coast route that snaked above verdant cliffs, and headed toward the sea.

The narrow road wound about a mile through the hillside hamlet of Laupāhoehoe, then dropped onto a small, bulbous peninsula. Marsue could scarcely believe her luck. It was the most idyllic place she had ever seen, an open landscape dotted with coconut trees and flanked by the towering cliffs on one side and a small cove on the other. The U-shaped school, set toward the back of the peninsula, was ringed with verandas and windows. It was built around a massive banyan tree whose branches dripped lazily toward the ground. From the classroom where she would teach high school art, Marsue looked out on a hedge of red hibiscus and beyond it a small, plumeriascented cemetery where a white horse grazed. The backdrop was a tableau of cliffs with glistening waterfall tendrils that dropped into the cove. Off in the distance, the snow-capped summit of the Mauna Kea volcano topped a lush vista. It was too perfect.

In fact, legend had it that the peninsula was born in far less tranquil circumstances, emerging from a rivalry between the snow goddess Poli'ahu and the volcano goddess Pele. The volatile Pele was said to have become so enraged at her foe that she launched a volcanic eruption, to which Poli'ahu responded with a snowstorm. The freezing winds blew the lava so that it swept down in a flow that created Laupāhoehoe Gulch and pushed into the sea to form the peninsula where the school now sat. But however tempestuous its origins, there was nothing in 1946 to indicate that Laupāhoehoe would be anything other than a wonderful place to live and work.

Five tidy wooden cottages in a straight row sat only steps from the rocky shoreline at the edge of the peninsula. Separated from the school by a large, grass playing field, these cottages were provided as living quarters for teachers. They were built in the Hawaiian style, on stilts a few feet off the ground. It had to be just about the best real estate anywhere. Marsue took up residence at one end of the row and met her roommates, three young women who shared her adventurous spirit. The four of them quickly bonded and developed big plans together. They would "teach around the world." Once they had their fill of Hawai'i, their next destination might be South America or Japan. In the meantime, they enjoyed their students, picnics at the beach, and the hospitality of people from the local sugar plantation.

◇◇◇

The four teachers were just stirring in their cottage shortly before 7 A.M. on April 1, a Monday. It was slightly rainy and breezy and just a bit cooler than the usual balmy temperatures. Marsue and her friends could hear the nearby playground swings creaking with children whose parents dropped them off early on the way to work at the sugar plantation. The women were upbeat, eager to get through this week and start their spring vacation. They planned a holiday in Honolulu, a reprise of the whirlwind Christmas trip that was still fresh in their minds. They had stayed at the Moana Hotel in Waikīkī and gloried in the availability of men, music, and dancing. Back in Laupāhoehoe, Marsue had been dating the plantation doctor, Leabert Fernandez, an athletic, dark-haired man who always wore a bow tie when he made his rounds at his three plantation hospitals. He was thirteen years her senior. Their good times had led to a deepening relationship, but Marsue had no thoughts of marriage. She had plans to teach around the world.

"Come see tidal wave!"

It was young Danny Akiona, whose family lived in the only house on the point besides the teachers' cottages. This sounded interesting. Marsue's image of a tidal wave, the misnomer that eventually would give way to the term tsunami, was from Hollywood—the towering mountain of water that crashed down and slurped up everything in its path. However, the subject of tsunamis, tidal waves, had never come up during her eight months in Hawai'i. Two tsunamis had visited Hawai'i in the early 1920s, but the last one that caused any significant destruction had been in the previous century.

Marsue was unaware that Hawai'i was vulnerable to earthquake fault zones around the Pacific Ocean. Earthquakes on these faults could trigger tsunamis, series of long waves launched when water is displaced by disturbance on the sea floor—whether volcanic eruption, landslide, or earthquake. Numerous tsunamis had hit Hawai'i in years past, crossing the ocean at jet speeds. On the open sea, tsunami waves were not visible, but when they slowed near coastline contours at places like Laupāhoehoe, they could become destructive. The compressed wave energy forced the water to rise and rush inland like a powerful, unstoppable tide, able to toss eight-ton boulders, uproot massive trees, and knock out railroad ties. Although Marsue, like many people, envisioned tsunamis as monster waves cresting high above the shoreline, a tsunami wave actually approaches land with the appearance of a rapidly rising wall of water. In later years, Hawai'i would develop a tsunami warning system, using sophisticated equipment to monitor faraway ocean changes. But in 1946, no system was in place.

Marsue and her three friends donned bathrobes and slippers and walked a short distance to a small rise where they could look down on the cove. There they saw the strange sucking and surging, like a bathtub draining and filling, Marsue thought. There was no towering surf. They looked at one another. So this was a tidal wave? Unimpressed, they turned back to the cottage, but the sea retreated again. Well here was something different—a twin tidal wave! Now this would be worth writing home about, Marsue thought. This time the incoming wave climbed higher onshore and deposited marine debris well above the high-tide mark.

The water was not moving especially fast, but it washed flopping fish and *naupaka* plants all over the school's playing field, even lapping underneath the teacher cottages. Kids by now were exploring the seabed and cavorting in the debris on the field above. Fred Kruse, the strapping, tall science teacher, came on the scene and herded a group of his students down into the newly exposed ocean floor for a rare chance to examine its bounty.

Marsue and her friends figured the start of school would probably be delayed this morning because of the mess. They returned to the cottage and quickly dressed. Marsue donned blue jeans and a heavy red-and-black-checked wool shirt, bought during a summer in Maine. She pulled on socks and saddle shoes. She expected she'd be doing some dirty clean-up work around the school. Her dark brown hair was still up in bobby pin curls that she labored over every night to create stylish waves. She tied a bandana around the bobby pins, then went onto the porch with Fay to shoot some photos. About thirty minutes had passed since Danny had brought the first alert.

Neither Marsue nor anyone else at Laupāhoehoe knew that earlier that morning, in the Aleutian Islands, 2,300 miles to the north, an offshore earthquake had rocked the remote lighthouse on Unimak Island. It was a big quake, registering 7.1 on the open-ended Richter scale. Within fifty minutes, waves towering more than one hundred feet bashed into the island and obliterated the lighthouse. Scientists later theorized that the quake also triggered a landslide, creating an even greater underwater disturbance. The displaced water began to move in giant waves across the Pacific. Seismographic equipment at the University of Hawai'i and the Hawai'i Volcano Observatory had registered the Aleutian quake. But no one yet realized that the powerful waves were rolling toward the islands, and that in a mere five hours they would hit with terrifying force, the most destructive tsunami in Hawai'i's history.

With a roar, the wave smashed through the teachers' cottage as if it were a pile of twigs. The women fought to keep their heads above water. Marsue felt Helen going down next to her. She put her hand under Helen's arm, but her friend was jerked from her grasp and swept away. Marsue grabbed the roof as it separated from the house. She was afloat, she and Fay clambering up the roof as it spun and tipped. They clung to their perch, and the wave began to recede again.

The water also blasted through the other cottages, knocking them back across the playing field toward the school building. A kitchen detached from one, ferrying its four teacher occupants clear up on the field, where it docked itself. A brown car belonging to the principal went spinning by Marsue and Fay, like a tinker toy tossed in a boiling pot. As the water sucked out again, the two women felt themselves moving rapidly, topsy-turvy toward the ocean.

Marsue saw a head bobbing by the corner of the roof. It was Dorothy. Marsue called to her. But Dorothy's eyes were wild and panicked, her body in the water, her hands grasping the edge of the roof. In the next second, her hands slid quickly off the edge and without a word, Dorothy disappeared into the potboil, sucked away so quickly that it was as if she had never been there at all.

Marsue had no time to grasp the horror of what she had seen. She felt a lurch and a clunk. She looked down and saw that the roof had lodged on a rock outcrop that had stopped them from whirling out to sea. With few words, the two women quickly assessed the situation. The waves would most certainly continue to surge. They had one chance—to race across the seabed and make it to higher ground before the next one struck. They scurried down and began picking their way as fast as they could manage across the seaweed and rocks. The carbon-colored rocks were sharp, some rising up like spires, others strewn in broken rubble, and hard to navigate. The women covered about forty feet. The water was on them in a whoosh.

Marsue, a strong swimmer, took a large breath as she was pushed under and slammed against the rocks. Debris and boulders were everywhere, pummeling and scraping her beneath the surface. She tried to push up but was powerless against the force of the water.

I'm going to die, she thought.

Time slowed down and her mind was consumed with a startling revelation. She was not praying. She had no thoughts of God. She had always been an atheist. And now confronted by death, she remained a nonbeliever. Friends, especially soldiers who had been in foxholes, had always told her that in a moment near death, faith would surely come to her. But here it was, and still she thought religion was a bunch of baloney. How frustrating it was to have this insight here beneath the water, where she could tell no one that she had been right all along.

Her chest ached from holding her breath. Her lungs were ready to explode. She could not hold on. But she became aware of white bubbles above her. She opened her mouth and broke the surface, gasping. After one frantic gulp of air, she was pushed under again. Once more, her lungs were taxed to bursting. This time, the water released her. Her head was up. She sucked the moist air. She was alive. Nearby was the small lighthouse that stood at the edge of the sea. It was covered to its roof in water. Floating, Marsue took stock, indulging in her first seconds of relative calm. Her jeans had been ripped away, along with her socks and shoes. She still wore her lumberjack shirt. She moved her legs, her arms. They seemed okay. She would survive this. Surrounded by wreckage, she grabbed the first substantial piece of wood that floated by, and then traded it for a bigger one.

The current was moving her along the coast. There was no point trying to get to land. Even if she could cross the rough waters, there was no beach or landing point. The rocky cliffs at the water's edge were impossible to climb and they extended for miles without a beachhead. She surely would be battered by the mass of floating objects if she tried to go ashore. She'd be better off floating with the swift current to the next possible landing spot—a sugar mill about twenty miles away. But certainly, she thought, with all the military and fishing boats in Hawai'i, she soon would be rescued. For a moment, she was seized by fear of sharks and other sea creatures. But no, she reasoned, there was so much junk in the water that predators couldn't possibly maneuver. There was rubbish floating everywhere: *hala* trees, shiny green *naupaka* plants, wood, furniture, canned goods, pillows, somebody's purse, all bobbing around in a giant seawater stew.

She snagged a door that came her way and draped herself across it. Her new raft slid up one side of the waves and down the other as the current swept her along. She saw people standing atop the cliffs. They looked so tiny and far away. She raised herself on the door, buttoned up her lumberjack shirt, and waved her arms wildly. There was no indication they saw her. They'd never notice her in all this junk, she thought. A chilly rain fell. Hours passed. Marsue was cold, desperately and repeatedly seasick, bruised and aching. Across the water she saw schoolboys on a raft of trees and boards. She couldn't reach them across the waves. They looked strangely white. Later she learned one had found a can of Crisco and smeared it on himself to protect his skin. Eventually, another teenage boy floated near, clinging to part of a tree. Marsue got her door close enough on a wave crest to speak to him. He pointed to a ship visible on the horizon.

"I go to ship," he said. "Nobody knows we're here."

Marsue told him it was too far to swim, too great a risk. But the boy doubted they could ever get to shore and safely land.

"I go to ship."

He slid from sight down the side of a wave. He was never seen again.

It was getting late. About 5 P.M., a small plane circled above Marsue.

"I'm alive!" she yelled, waving her arms.

The plane flew away. The pilot hadn't seen her, she thought, despairing. But soon the plane came back, circled, and dropped a package—far away from Marsue. That must mean others were still out here with her. The aircraft dropped a second package that came close to Marsue's floating door, a yellow bundle with a large handle and the word "Pull." She yanked. A tiny raft inflated itself. Bone-drenching relief flooded Marsue's battered body. She pulled herself over the side and collapsed. For the first time in more than nine hours she no longer had to cling to a thin piece of wood for survival. She leaned back. It was almost relaxing. She dug into one of the pockets lining the sides of the raft and found a fishing line. Not much chance she'd be fishing, she mused.

Dusk was coming, the waves still big and rough. She looked up to see the boat nearly upon her, a smallish pond boat with its aft section cut to accommodate an outboard motor. There leaning over the side, amazingly, was Leabert, her doctor beau! With boats up and down the coast destroyed by the tsunami, Fernandez had hunted down a boat on the other side of the island, certain that he could find survivors and treat them as needed. After working with another man to adapt the boat for the motor, Fernandez and a crew of three picked up two boys clinging to a floating tree branch. One had a serious head wound that Fernandez bandaged. Fernandez had dared to hope that Marsue would be out here somewhere. He was elated to find her safe.

"Now you'll have to marry me," he told her as he bundled her in blankets.

The news from Laupāhoehoe was not as promising. Marsue's three housemates were lost. All three women were adherents to religious faith, but they were gone and she had survived, she thought ruefully. They were among 158 victims throughout Hawai'i, twenty-four of them at Laupāhoehoe, including Mr. Kruse and his students who had explored the sea bottom. Some schoolchildren had raced to the bleachers on their playing field and climbed up to escape the rushing water. As the largest of the eight tsunami waves roared in at more than thirty feet high, the structure collapsed and the children were swept away. The town of Hilo, twenty-five miles down the coast, was devastated. Buildings were smashed and people were tossed into the bay, never to be seen again. In some spots the water had penetrated more than a half mile inland. Some places saw as much as five hundred feet of sea floor exposed by the drainage between waves. The April Fool's Day disaster was one of thirteen significant tsunamis that would hit the Hawaiian Islands in the twentieth century, all of them sparked by Pacific earthquakes.

Back at Laupāhoehoe, Fernandez' boat slid carefully into shore, guided through the darkness by a local man who knew the coast well. Marsue and the two boys were driven up the hill to the hospital, where on typical days, Fernandez would be caring for plantation patients. Lining the narrow road were townspeople who peered anxiously into the car, straining in the darkness to see if their loved ones might be the survivors in the back seat. Eyes filled with fading hope bored into an exhausted Marsue. She never forgot those faces.

Bruised, but without serious injuries, Marsue spent a few days in the hospital recuperating. Adjusting to the deeper changes brought by the tsunami, giving up the world travel plans she had shared with her friends, took longer. She married Fernandez that summer. By then, she had returned to her teaching, finishing the school year with the other tsunami survivors. With many school desks empty and faculty members lost forever, there was a pall over the little school that had grown from a single room three decades earlier. The education department eventually closed it down, leaving only the banyan tree that would live out the century and beyond. The school had suffered no more than water damage, but nobody wanted to send their children there. They opened a new school on the other side of the coast road—on higher ground.

Six years after the tsunami, Marsue and her husband left Laupāhoehoe for Honolulu, where Marsue continued her teaching. They later divorced, and Marsue married John McShane in 1969. Now retired, she lives at the beach on Oʻahu. She still has her red lumberjack shirt, a souvenir of her tsunami ordeal.

Laupāhoehoe, 2003

Marsue McShane, Lanikai, 2003

Inside Nature's Washing Machine

Brian Keaulana and Craig Davidson knew this cave. At the base of a twenty-foot cliff, it was formed by volcanic lava that had hardened, black and jagged, where it flowed into the sea more than a million years earlier. The cave sat at the back of an inlet scooped from the rocky coastline. Locals called this place the Moi Hole, after a native fish found in that area. The cave absorbed waves so forceful that when they crashed against the cliff they sometimes sprayed like geysers forty feet above the ledge where tourists would stand, swamping the cliff. The ocean rushed straight into that cave and blasted around its walls before rocketing back to sea.

Keaulana and Davidson, water safety officers who patrolled the coast in their Yamaha Waverunner watercraft, had practiced and visualized rescues all along this west side of O'ahu. They knew that when the surf was high, the Moi Hole was one nasty trap. A person could get badly battered in there by the powerful pounding of wave against rock. The Moi Hole was a washing machine, filled with tons of water that swirled crazily, then spat back out to sea. You didn't want to get caught in that cave.

On January 25, 1993, the two lifeguards were on duty at Mākaha Beach on the west side of Oʻahu, one of Hawaiʻi's most famous surfing spots. Bronzed and fit, they looked every bit the heroic protectors of hapless beachgoers. Guys like Brian and Craig who had grown up at the beach had water skills that actually fit the tourist image of a native Hawaiian. This day they were busy with run-of-the-mill beach rescues in rough surf. Waves were as high as thirty feet at the face, and they had dispatched another lifeguard team to help out over on the North Shore, where the real monster waves were in season. A call came over the radio about a "swimmer in distress" at Yokohama Bay, some ten minutes from Mākaha. The two men climbed aboard their Waverunner and sped up the coast. Probably a swimmer got swept out and needed to be plucked from the current, Keaulana thought.

When they arrived, the beach was quiet, but they saw people gathered on a ledge beyond the far edge of the sand.

Oh god, it's the Moi Hole, thought Craig.

A fire department crew and Yokohama Beach lifeguards stood on the ledge, pointing down into a foamy, churning cauldron that was surging in and out of the inlet. Waves crashed against the cliff and rained down on them.

"A man washed over the side," the guys on shore shouted to Brian and Craig.

Brian peered into the turbulence, darting the Waverunner back and forth. No sign of anybody. Nothing. He needed to find out what the wave had done with its conquest. There was one good way to do that. Grabbing a mask, and already wearing fins, Brian jumped in. Crazy, maybe, for a less competent person. But Brian was confident in his knowledge of the ocean. The current pushed him straight to the mouth of the cave. The scary truth hit him—this guy was stuck inside one of the most fearsome places on the island, a nightmare come true. He made it back to the Waverunner and waited for a lull. Then he and Craig edged the watercraft to the cave opening. The water was so high when the surge came up that they could almost touch the ceiling. The two lifeguards could see nothing in the darkness. But they heard a voice:

"Help me!"

◇◇◇

The day had started out perfectly for Hugh Alexander, a sandy-haired, twenty-six-year-old attorney from San Francisco who had brought his girlfriend Katja Teip to Hawai'i for three days of fun and romance. He was determined to impress this smart, pretty young woman, and in that regard the trip was going extremely well. They were guests of Hugh's family friend, Michael Moran, at his home in the elegant Diamond Head neighborhood of O'ahu. The trio blended sightseeing with relaxation and Waikīkī nightlife. They had a wonderful time, and Hugh was more smitten with Katja than ever. On this last day of the trip, they had gone diving, reveling in the colorful reef life. They drove across the island to see the big waves on the North Shore, and then decided to head up the coast beyond Mākaha. At Yokohama Beach, they got out to photograph the tempestuous surf, then strolled to the rocky cliffs for a more dramatic vantage point. A small sign warned DANGER WAVES ON LEDGE. Someone was fishing off to the side. The uneven surface of broad ledge was wet and puddled, and seawater was spraying up above the cliff. Not much of a daredevil, Hugh stayed several feet back from the edge as he eyed the ferocious rocks below. It all looked pretty scary.

He and Katja positioned themselves so that Michael could take their picture with the waves spraying behind them. Water surged onto the cliff like a pot of potatoes boiling over, then ran in foamy rivulets down the sides. Side by side, Hugh and Katja grinned for the photo. Then came the sound of an explosion. Hugh heard it but had no time to react before water was cascading down on him, whacking his calves and knocking his feet from under him. Instinctively, he reached his arm behind him as he toppled backward. His effort to brace the fall sent a stab of pain through his wrist. The arm twisted on the rock as his head hit the ground.

Katja was on her knees leaning over him.

"I think I broke my arm," he said.

She thought he was kidding. "Oh, come on," she teased.

In an instant another blast was upon them. Hugh was immediately underwater this time, sliding quickly toward the side where the Moi Hole yawned. Thinking of the rocks below, he grasped at the ground with both arms, panicky. The water was carrying him fast now. His mind zoomed. He was going over backwards; his head would hit the rocks! But the water in the cove was rising fast. He tumbled into the powerful swirl. Mercifully, the rising cauldron cushioned what would have been a long, headfirst drop onto the rocks below. Hugh looked up and saw his friend Michael running on the ledge, horror sweeping across his face. He was racing to Katja, who had fallen but was not swept in.

Hugh was filled with terror. This was it. And how strange, he found himself thinking, that death could come so early, before he had a chance to do the things a person should do with his life. He had just begun practicing law. He had accomplished nothing, he thought, and it was all going to end here in a Hawaiian idyll suddenly turned into a nightmare.

Another swell grabbed him and yanked him beneath the water, then whacked him against a rock wall. Now he was up again, inside a cave, then completely submerged, pushed down, twisting under wild surges of water that smashed him into rocks the size of wastebaskets. He wasn't going to make it. Somehow, he saw a hole in the back wall of the cave, maybe thirty yards away. He had to get to that hole, or be thrashed repeatedly against the sharp cave walls. He started toward it. Another wave blasted in, a runaway train crashing into a mouse tunnel. It hit the back wall, taking Hugh with it and battering him again against tumbling boulders. The water receded. He was on a tiny spit of sand at the top of the cave, stunned, leaning onto his right side. Hugh started to gasp and cry, blood and salt water trickling down his face.

What's going on? he thought.

Water surged into the cave again, but less powerfully. He snapped to. He was in a cave. He had to hang on before the next wave hit. He splashed over to a large boulder and grabbed it in a bear hug. The next explosion hit, flung him off the rock, and yanked him again to the back of the cave, swirled and scraped anew. He could see the hole. He flung himself to it and crawled in on all fours. It was a cubicle about as big as the leg space under his office desk. Hugh had room to dig in his heels and push his back up against the top. When the next wave rocketed in, he held his breath, pushing up to brace himself as the hole filled with water. His back was painfully lacerated, but at least he was no longer smacked around in the deafening mael-strom.

This is not a situation I can get out of, he thought.

But it was such a cold, horrible, violent place to be. His scrapes and cuts were bleeding. What if sharks came?

He needed to figure out a way to get past that mountain of water that blocked his freedom. Perhaps he could hold onto boulders along the side of the cave and work his way out. He left the hole and gave it a try, but was slammed back by the next merciless wave. He sat back down in the hole.

Brian Keaulana knew perhaps better than anyone what Hugh was up against. Keaulana was one of Hawai'i's most respected watermen, famous in lifeguard circles for his valor and knowledge of the ocean. He had grown up on the beach, the son of surfing champion and lifeguarding legend Buffalo Keaulana, a fixture in the community. Like his dad, Brian was a competitive surfer and an expert on cur-rents and ocean survival. He was always studying the ocean and working on new lifesaving strategies. Eventually he would become a water safety consultant for movies and a stuntman in dangerous water scenes.

Brian also was a pioneer in using personal watercraft for life-guarding. The idea had come to him when he experienced a major wipeout during a big-wave surfing contest. He had popped to the sur-face that day to see a friend checking on him from a traditional stand-up Jet Ski. Brian was in trouble, but there was no way the per-sonal watercraft could pluck him from the water. A wave the size of an apartment building crashed down on his head. He survived the experience, but started thinking: there had to be a better way to adapt those watercraft to whisk people to safety, to shave time off the typical lifesaving methods that utilized surfboards and rescue tubes.

He immediately set to work, purchasing a Yamaha Waverunner and lashing a bodyboard-type sled to the back. Now the perfected version of that craft was a standard rescue tool. It allowed a lifeguard to reach a victim in under two minutes, for instance, compared with the twenty minutes it might take to paddle a surfboard the same distance. Brian trained other lifeguards in use of the watercraft. His philosophy was that ocean safety didn't require fear of the water. It was all about knowledge and respect, and the Moi Hole was certainly a place that demanded no less.

Twenty-six years earlier, Brian's father had performed a fabled rescue in this same cave. It was long before the days of motorized rescue craft, and three people were trapped. Fearlessly, Buffalo had paddled a surfboard into the cave and pulled out two boys. Before he could return for the man still hollering from inside, the surf rose to block the cave entrance. He retrieved the body the next day when the surf dropped.

The lifeguards had discussed that very rescue a couple of weeks earlier in a workshop that Brian led on worst-case scenarios. The participants had brainstormed about what they would do, even raising ideas like drilling into the cave from above, a desperate ploy but one that showed what they all knew: venturing into that cave in boiling surf could mean death for even the strongest swimmer. Brian understood that getting out would be challenging, if not impossible. In Hugh's position, even an experienced waterman probably would give up, knowing the futility of fighting the angry ocean against such odds, Brian later said. But Hugh didn't know the magnitude of what he was up against.

At twenty-one, Craig Davidson was ten years younger than Brian, a comparative rookie on the lifeguarding staff. This was Craig's first big rescue. He had grown up around lifeguard role models who had taken him under their wings. He admired Brian, was in awe of his courage, instinct, and knowledge. In later years, he would join Brian in stuntman work. But with just two years on the lifeguarding staff, Craig knew it would be awhile before he could reach his mentor's standard of accomplishment.

Coincidentally, only a week or so earlier, when the sea was much calmer, he had explored the Moi Hole with another lifeguard, surveying ways to get in and out—just in case. Craig considered this one of the most dangerous places on the island. He wanted to stay optimistic about the rescue, but from the moment he heard Hugh's cry for help and saw the size of the surf, he felt that he and Brian would be bringing out a body.

Now the two lifeguards were energized by the sound of Hugh's voice, and automatically went into full rescue mode, using all their training to maximize their efforts. They zoomed the Waverunner in and out of the cove, aided by hand signals and whistles from the emergency workers onshore who could see wave sets advancing behind them. Brian hovered each time at the cave mouth, knowing that if they got caught in the inlet by an incoming wave, they would be crashed into the cave along with their watercraft. Inside the cave, the water rose to within a few feet of the ceiling, leaving the prospect that the Waverunner could be slammed against it by the wild waters. The lifeguards yelled for Hugh to come out where they could grab him. If they swam in for him, they could be trapped, too.

In one pass, they lingered seconds too long near the cave

entrance. The retreating wave sucked out to reveal a huge rock in the middle of the inlet. They made a run for the open ocean, but too late. The Waverunner was pulled into the rock and swamped. They lost power. The two lifeguards jumped overboard and began kicking and pushing until they had swum the craft out beyond the surf. A Fire Department helicopter was called to tow it to nearby Yokohama Beach. Craig rode along with it, while Brian waited for a backup watercraft.

Brian was nowhere near giving up on this rescue. During a lull in wave sets, and despite the danger, he decided to have another look in the cave. From shore, his friends signaled that he had two minutes to swim in and out before the next wave set. Inside the cave there was no sign of Hugh.

He must be somewhere at the back, Brian thought.

Up top, he heard his friends urgently whistling. A big set was rushing toward him. He dashed for the cave entrance, but ran into the surge that was pushing in. He was swimming, with all his strength, at a standstill. He knew what to do. He gulped a huge breath of air and dove for the bottom, finding rocks and reef that he could grab. The wave exploded all around. He clung to the bottom until his fingers felt as if they would be yanked from his hands. But he knew that the wave energy now pulling at him eventually had to go back out. If he could hang on, the undercurrent would help him out. His life hinged on staying calm and using all of his experience with the ocean. He was trained to hold his breath for long periods of time. Relaxing, not panicking, was vitally important, as Brian always emphasized in his water safety classes. That was the key to ocean survival. Surfers who weathered huge wipeouts, buried under tons of cascading water, knew this crucial strategy. You couldn't fight the ocean currents. It was useless to try. You had to wait, and use the current to carry you away from danger.

Now Brian stayed as low as he could, keeping his body close to the contour of the bottom to prevent the power of the water from whipping him back. If he let up, he'd be slammed. On the bottom he had a chance. It seemed forever until he felt the slight push from the forefront of the surge coming out. He let go and went with it, all the way outside the inlet to deep water. He popped up and gulped for air. The harrowing experience confirmed that there was no way he could swim in and grab the tourist. This was going to be up to Hugh.

◈◈◈

Hugh was running his stopwatch inside the cave. He had waited twenty minutes before he started yelling for help. Now forty minutes had passed, and he didn't know if anyone was out there. It was deafening in the darkness of the cave, every wave arriving with the fury and sound of a bomb. He needed to make a swim for it, he thought, in case there were rescuers. He tried twice to dash for the mouth of the cave. Each time he was thrown back. He worried about breaking his limbs. He tried again, this time diving for the bottom and then swimming underwater with the surge going out. He popped up in the inlet, blinded by the sudden sunshine. Screaming drifted over the roar that filled his ears. But he couldn't make out the shouts, or see anyone. His head was barely above the water before the roiling surf dragged him under and pummeled him against the cliff. Someone threw a rescue tube. He tried to grab it. He felt himself flipped upside down and pulled under for a long time.

I can't find the top, he thought. *I'm going to die.*

He needed to breathe. He was out of time. He opened his mouth, sure of death. He felt air rush in. He was back in the explosive cave again. But he had seen the Waverunner outside. Now he knew that if he could just make it out of the cave, there was someone to grab him.

◇◇◇

The backup Waverunner had arrived at the beach a short distance from the Moi Hole, but beyond view of the inlet. Brian went to retrieve it and asked lifeguard Earl Bungo to be his partner. Earl was a low-key local guy, big, tough, and powerful, and one of the most knowledgeable and athletic of their elite lifeguard corps. Earl would ride on the rescue sled attached to the Waverunner. If Hugh came out, Earl would grab him and drag him onto the sled, then fling himself prone on top of Hugh to keep him from slipping off. As Brian and Earl pulled the Waverunner up to the inlet, everyone was shouting. Hugh was out! But the waves were upon him.

"Dive! dive!" they yelled to him.

Brian had spotted Hugh's head in the whirlpool and steered on top of the first wave. He didn't have time to reach him. He and Earl screamed at Hugh to dive down. If he could get to the undercurrent, he could ride it out. But the water engulfed him and whisked him back to the cave. Brian could hear the sound of Hugh's flesh, slapped and scraped on the rocks.

Like a piece of steak being pounded, he thought. *He's going to die.*

Brian hoped Hugh didn't grab the rescue tube that was bobbing crazily into the cave. Safety at this point was underneath the water, not on top. Buoyancy would only help the water bang Hugh around the cave. The lifeguards wanted the tube out of there.

Now it was Earl's turn to go in. Earl jumped into the water and swam to the cave. He retrieved the rescue tube, but didn't see Hugh. When he came out, he had his own safety to worry about, pounded as he was by waves in the seconds before Brian was able to pluck him from the water. Now the two rescuers darted the Waverunner in and out of the inlet, praying Hugh would make another try and that they would be there at the right instant. Brian repeatedly zoomed to the cave entrance, pivoted and backed up to the mouth, positioning the craft for a rapid exit.

"Where are you? What side?" they hollered into the roar. From the depths of the cave came only the echo of exploding waves.

It looked hopeless, but there was still a chance Hugh could make it. He was alive when they last saw him. He had survived this long. They would be ready if he reappeared. They talked about what they would do, knowing their own lives were in peril.

"The worst that can happen," Brian told Earl, "is that I lose you to the cave, too, or that both of us get sucked in and trashed with the Waverunner."

They had little room to maneuver, but their watercraft was like a surgeon's tool. Given the chance, they could use it to save a life. Brian later would reflect on this as the hairiest rescue of his life, but at the moment he and Earl were too intent on their task to be overwhelmed by the enormity of their challenge. They could hold back to ensure their own safety, but their professionalism pushed them in the opposite direction. They were determined to save this man they had never met, and that thought overrode every distraction. If they did grab Hugh, they knew the waves could still wipe him and Earl from the sled. So Earl donned a rescue tube and connected it to a line from the Waverunner, a backup strategy that would allow Brian to drag them to safety if they were dumped from the sled.

Time was slipping by with no sign of Hugh.

The rising tide might be a problem, Brian thought.

But more frightening was that the surf itself was growing, engulfing the cave as it surged in. Although Hawai'i's waters are warm, Hugh faced the threat of hypothermia inside the chilly cave.

◇◇◇

Hugh crouched in his hole, his mind wandering. He needed his strength to go out again. He tried to focus on escape. He told himself he was just a big baby because he wasn't yet out there again challenging the force that pinned him here. He should simply relax and go. At the same time he was petrified that death was near. He thought of family and friends he would miss, his brother, sister, parents. How sad they would be if he did not make it home. He didn't want them to go through that. Absently, he stuck his hand into the pocket of his baggy green shorts.

The rental car keys! Holy smokes, this had meaning. The keys were still with him. He should tie them onto the drawstring of his shorts to secure them. No, that would be cocky, he reasoned, the equivalent of telling God that he knew he would definitely survive. That might doom his chances by making it seem that he had no humility. Better to leave it to God's will, but try to keep the keys just in case. He twisted them into the fabric in his pocket, making them a little more secure but not invulnerable.

He interrupted this reverie to look at his watch. He was stunned: an hour and a half had passed since he had swum out of the cave. He was cold. He must be delirious, probably hypothermic, he thought. He told himself to snap out of it. The water was higher now, no longer receding for him to breathe. Between sets he had to leave the hole and stick his head above water at the top of the cave. When he felt the next wave inbound, he'd duck under water and go back to the hole, holding his breath. He had to get out of here. Soon.

Just go now, now, now, he told himself.

As he was preparing to make his move, his footing slipped. A wave that was sucking out of the cave grabbed him and swept him to the mouth. He had to go for it. He dove for the bottom, then swam out using all his remaining strength.

◇◇◇

It was a bad moment. A big set was about to break. For Brian and Earl, however, the die was cast. When they saw Hugh surging out, they knew this was their last chance. They had to make an attempt to grab him no matter what.

"Hang on!" Brian shouted to Earl.

He sped in front of the wave that was hurtling toward the cave. It was already breaking as he raced it to the middle of the inlet where Hugh bobbed with his arm outstretched. Brian swung toward him, pivoting to face the wave as he flung Earl in Hugh's direction. The two men lunged for each other, and Earl clutched Hugh, shoving him onto the rescue sled. At full speed, Brian punched toward the top of the wave that coiled above them. They needed every ounce of power and momentum to keep the Waverunner from tipping back toward the cave. Brian shot over the top with the mountain of surf crashing around them. A cheer rose from the cliffs.

The exuberance trailed off as the wave knocked both Earl and Hugh off the sled, floating free but still tethered to the Waverunner. Earl screamed in pain. Hugh had his arm in a death vise. A second wave was coming fast, but Brian knew they were safe. He yanked them taut to the edge of the cove, then let the rope go slack as he circled back. With one hand on the controls, he leaned down and with his free hand powerfully hoisted the two men onto the sled. Hugh was beneath Earl, who yelled in his face, "We got you! We got you!"

Brian Keaulana turned to his comrades on shore. He pumped his fist skyward in triumph. Then he sped the Waverunner to the nearby beach.

Craig Davidson was onshore with the rescue team. When Hugh was brought to the sand for oxygen and emergency care, Craig thought the young tourist looked like he'd been on the losing end of a street fight, with cuts everywhere, slicing his face, head, and torso. No one could believe that Hugh had survived the ordeal inside the Moi Hole, including the men who risked their own lives to save him. Hugh had no broken bones, but required multiple stitches on his head and face. He didn't know why he had been allowed to survive. All he knew was that two men had faced death themselves, with a bravery he could scarcely comprehend, to gift him with the rest of his life. That, and also that when he reached into his pocket, the rental car keys were still there.

Hugh Alexander returned to San Francisco to practice law. He and Katja went their separate ways. He married and began working his way through a list of things he wanted to do in life. One was returning to see the Moi Hole. Brian Keaulana, Craig Davidson, and Earl Bungo received the Medal of Valor, Hawai'i's highest lifeguarding award, for their actions.

Hugh Alexander, 2003. Photo courtesy of Hugh Alexander.

Throat of the Earth

It's pitch dark down here. Peter Paton looked around groggily. *Must be nighttime,* he thought.

He didn't remember falling, and now his head was too thick to contemplate what had happened to him. But he obviously had stumbled into an earth crack and had been asleep down here. He was sore, listing onto his side. It hurt to sit up. Maybe he could stand and try to pull himself out. He hoisted himself up a bit, and immediately felt weak and lightheaded. He quickly slumped back down. He didn't hear any birds singing. In fact, he couldn't hear anything at all. He couldn't see a thing either, not even stars. It was probably the middle of the night, a cloudy night, and he figured he was at the bottom of a crack that was several feet over his head. He would wait until first light and then pull himself out.

◈◈◈

It had started as an easy day on the bird survey. Paton, a biologist with the U.S. Fish and Wildlife Service, was part of an ambitious, multiyear project to count and categorize Hawai'i's bird population, the largest ever survey of its kind. The goal was to learn which species were endangered and to catalog those and other birds. Since the advent of Polynesians and Europeans, half of Hawai'i's 149 native bird species had been lost to extinction, with many more now endangered. Alarm was spreading through wildlife circles. The islands had lost more native bird life than any other part of the world. Now, the surveyors would map the distribution of species and try to learn how nonnative birds affected the indigenous species. The team was nearing the end of its work on the Big Island of Hawai'i, where they trudged through terrain that ranged from lush rain forest to dry fields of hardened lava. By the time the project concluded, they would produce a comprehensive survey of birds throughout the Hawaiian Islands.

The bird surveyors traipsed along transects, the mostly uncut trails that were marked by blue ribbons tied around the trees. They stopped at regular intervals where a red flag marked a survey spot. They would then count birds for eight minutes, recording the species on their clipboards. The surveyors rarely saw the birds, instead identifying them by sound. Like his colleagues, Peter had a flawlessly trained ear. He could recognize any bird species by its distinctive song or chatter. At twenty-three, he was fairly new to the bird crew, having come aboard about a month earlier, following a stint with the U.S. Forest Service in Hawai'i.

This day in June 1979 was unusual because Peter and his partner, Jack Jeffrey, would be entering and coming out of the backcountry on the same day instead of camping out two or more days as was typical. Their trailhead was within easy walking distance of a road near the Mauna Ulu lava flow of Hawai'i Volcanoes National Park, several miles south of the park's scenic Crater Rim Drive. The day started at first light, around 5:30 A.M. The birds were most vocal in the morning, and the surveyors would stay out about five hours.

Peter's partner was a fellow wildlife biologist and avid nature photographer who had been on the job for two years. Jack knew Peter as a new guy on the team who was clearly well-versed and had trained quickly. The two of them were to survey the lower part of the transect and meet up with Rich McArthur, who was starting at the top near the Thurston Lava Tube, a popular tourist attraction that took visitors into a black-walled tunnel formed by flowing lava that had cooled and hardened into a giant cylinder.

Jack and Peter dropped Rich off and then parked just a short hike away from their own starting point.

"Which way do you want to go?" Jack asked.

There were only two options. One of the men would go up the transect and meet Rich coming down from the Thurston Lava Tube. The other would walk to the opposite end and then retrace his steps to rejoin the other two where Peter and Jack stood now. They'd have some lunch on the trail before driving back to their headquarters.

Peter made his fateful decision.

"I guess I'll go down."

"See you in a few hours," Jack said.

It was a pleasant, dewy morning. The biologists wore their yellow rain jackets and pants, not because of rain, but because they were wading through wet vegetation. The trees here were mostly native 'ōhi'a scattered in a sparse forest, but the ground cover was a dense waist-to-chest-high canopy of *uluhe* fern that could soak them through. Often the ground was completely obscured by the aggressive, almost matted greenery. Peter tramped along at a brisk pace. There were not many endangered birds in this area, but his clipboard filled with a variety of other species. Deciphering every bleep, tweet, and trill, he jotted the names of *'apapane, 'i'iwi, 'elepaio,* and nonnative species of finch, cardinal, and Japanese white-eye as he moved from one blue flag to the next.

He spotted the next flag wrapped around a tree that was just up a rise. Without a thought, he marched toward it. It was no different from any other blue flag Peter had seen that morning. He didn't change his purposeful gait or think twice about his course. Nor did he see another flag off to the side that indicated the route was sweeping in an arc at this point instead of lining up directly to the flag Peter now had in front of him.

He was in midstride when time hiccupped. The *uluhe* ferns were clawing Peter head to toe with wet leaves. Just as quickly they slid upward away from him as gravity took him. His next reality was total darkness, his body crouched fetally, a mess of bloody scrapes, aches, and bruises.

◇◇◇

Jack Jeffrey had covered his section of the transect and reconnoitered with Rich. The two men walked back to where Peter and Jack had split up. They munched on their lunch while waiting. Forty-five minutes passed without Peter. They decided he must have finished ahead of them, but there was no sign of him at the car either. Puzzled but not particularly concerned, they waited another hour.

Now his absence seemed peculiar, but still not much cause for worry. Perhaps he grew tired of waiting and walked back to headquarters. It was a few miles up the road, but Peter liked to walk. They took a last look toward the trail, then drove back to the office. No one there had seen Peter. Now sensing a problem, they wondered if maybe he had hitchhiked home.

In the nearby town of Volcano, his housemate Laurie MacIvor said he hadn't shown up there either. Jack was worried now. He reported his partner's absence to Mike Scott, chief biologist for the Fish and Wildlife Service on the Big Island and their boss on the bird survey. This didn't sound good, Mike thought. It wasn't unheard of that a surveyor would get lost, but typically he would have found his way to a road and made contact by this time. Mike directed Jack and Rich to return to the transect and see if perhaps Peter was still trailing. Yelling Peter's name, the two retraced their route through the *uluhe*. They returned to Mike alarmed.

"We've got a problem," Mike said. "We've gotta find him."

Mike Scott trained his people to be aware of earth cracks. It was probably the biggest potential hazard for bird surveyors, since their work was conducted almost entirely off the regular trail system. This part of Hawai'i was riddled with cracks, crevices, and fissures, the result of earthquakes and volcanic activity over centuries. Lava tubes also dotted the landscape, formed by channels of flowing lava that built a crust where a top layer of molten rock chilled against the air and hardened. Lava continued to flow under the crust, eventually leaving behind a hollow, hard lava tube.

As to the earth cracks, they could be hundreds of yards long, or very short. They could be as thin as a pencil or several feet wide. They were simply a part of the terrain on the Big Island. Hikers cutting across trails, or even researchers and park workers, occasionally fell into these openings, especially where they were obscured by thick vegetation. Often, they were able to climb back out. But Mike had heard stories about people lost down the cracks outside the park, cracks so remote that search dogs had to be brought in to find them. Usually they were lucky enough to have companions who could help them or could phone for assistance. Everyone knew, however, that many cracks were of unknown depth, and if someone fell into one, it might as well be a bottomless fall because there would be no way of finding him.

It was already afternoon, and Mike knew the day would gobble up the time he needed to mobilize a search for Peter. He phoned the National Park Service rangers and called in all of his surveyors who were near enough to help search. He grabbed some gear—rescue packs with climbing tools, ropes, first aid. Mike didn't know what he might need. He threw the packs in his car and drove as close as he could get to the bottom of the transect near the Mauna Ulu lava flow, Peter's turnaround point.

Laurie MacIvor was really worried. Peter was her closest friend. They had met at Lewis and Clark College and immediately hit it off. It was not a romance, but the strongest friendship and compatibility that bound them. They shared a passion for birding and outdoor adventure, and together they had done their senior project on great blue herons, building a bird blind high in the trees to conduct their research. They both managed to get hired after graduation by the U.S. Forest Service in Hawai'i. They rented a house together and spent their free time exploring and enjoying the islands. Their nickname for each other was "Pal."

When she got the call on Saturday that her friend was missing, Laurie wanted to dash out and join the search team. She worked on the bird survey herself. She knew how easy it was to run into trouble in the wild. She had experienced the daydreamy feeling of strolling between counting stations in a reverie until a red flag announced it was time to stop and count. In thick jungle terrain, the surveyors sometimes had to take several compass readings between stations just to make sure they were going in the right direction. Bird survey work was more complex than it might seem. Still, Laurie had a conviction deep down that Peter was alive. Their connection was such that if he had not survived she believed she would have felt something. When Laurie asked to join the searchers, her superiors asked her to stay put in case Peter wandered in or called.

The searchers spread out arms-length apart and pushed into the forest. They looked for holes and cracks and yelled into every opening they saw. If Peter had stepped into a crack he might have broken his leg, hit his head or worse, leaving him unable to move. They turned up nothing. Soon it would be dusk and too dark to search, Mike thought. Nobody wanted to give up, but the fact was they'd have to call a halt soon. Mike looked up and saw a botanist from his team coming down the transect.

"What's the most problematic area up there?" Mike asked him.

The botanist cited a specific section with a proliferation of cracks. Mike and some of the others hiked up. They noticed a place just off the trail where the fern looked a little bit askew. Not really smashed, but just a little disturbed. The men parted the ferns, and there was a crack, some three feet across. Big enough for a person to step into and fall right through. Mike got down on the ground and peered into the yawning darkness. Shining a flashlight, he thought he saw a small flash of yellow a few yards down. He yelled into the crack. He couldn't be positive, but he thought he heard a muffled voice call back. A biologist on the crew, Jim Jacobi, an accomplished climber and outdoorsman, offered to lean into the hole if someone would anchor his legs. Mike held onto him and he dropped his head into the crack.

"Peter, are you in there?" he yelled.

There was a pause. From deep, deep in the crevice, a sound came back. Faint, muted, far away, but it was a voice. Then Jim glimpsed the bright yellow scrap that had to be a ragged strip of Peter's raincoat. The crew members began shouting into the hole. They were convinced that was Peter trying to answer them down there. As they cleared the ferns away from the hole, they had no idea how deep it was, only that Peter seemed almost beyond shouting distance. The park rangers broke out ropes and tied them around trees. Climbing harnesses, litters, and helmets were prepared. Lanterns lit the darkening forest.

Aside from his concern about Peter's fate—he worried that the young biologist might have broken his back—Mike Scott was of two minds about the fact that Peter was the one down there. On the one hand, Peter was in excellent shape. He had grown up an avid skier in Colorado, worked on ski patrol—had hiked to the top of Mount Hood in Oregon. During all their adventures together, Laurie had never seen Peter afraid. He had an outdoorsman's confidence and versatility, just the kind of person you'd want to have with you if you got into trouble. Mike thought Peter might well have the skills and physical conditioning to survive this. But in another sense, he felt Peter was the worst guy who could be down in this crack because he was the most capable to help rescue someone else. They would need climbers to descend into the crack and people to work the ropes up top, belaying those who went down, not to mention medical staff. As it turned out, the group now assembled around the crack proved up to the task in every way.

The chief ranger, Chris Cameron, looked around at the group of rangers and bird surveyors, biologists and botanists. Who would volunteer to go down the hole? No one doubted it would be dangerous duty. Dropping into the darkness of the earth's intestines with only a skinny rope for security wasn't something to be taken lightly. Rappelling was part of park rangers' training, but they trained over regular cliffs. Nobody really went down into these unpredictable cracks. There could be steam at the bottom and there was always a chance the earth would shift while someone was in there. As the chill of the night closed in, two rangers, Brian Goring and Larry Katahira, spoke up. They'd go for Peter.

Larry peered over the edge. He knew there would be loose rocks on the way down, and therein would lie most of the danger. He'd lost hunting dogs down these cracks while out tracking wild pigs. It wasn't easy to get anything out of these crevices. Rocks, even boulders, could shake loose from the sides when disturbed by a boot or a rope, posing serious risk for both Peter and the rescuers. Not to mention that this wasn't a straight-down tunnel. Larry could see that it zigzagged. Peter must have bounced his way down, hitting the sides.

Larry and Brian climbed into their rappelling gear and harnesses, with headlamps on their hardhats. They carried backpacks with water, radios, a first aid kit, and a helmet for Peter. They would secure him in a soft-sided litter or harness, depending on his condition, and would hook him to a rope to be hoisted out.

❖❖❖

On his shelf, Peter was still dazed. He felt something warm oozing onto his body, unaware that it was blood from a head injury. His arms and legs didn't seem to be broken, but he was weak and hurting. It had not occurred to him that he wouldn't be able to get out on his own. If he could only get some sleep, he thought, he'd get out of here in the morning. He couldn't be more than a few feet down. He heard his name being called from far away. He recognized Mike Scott's voice. He tried to call back.

❖❖❖

The descent was painstaking, scary, awful. For most of it, Larry and Brian were in a chute big enough to freefall. But there were narrow parts where they could touch the walls on both sides. They clung to their ropes with gloved hands. The guys up top would lower them a bit and stop, then lower them again, communicating by yelling back and forth, as well as by radio. They dropped twenty feet, thirty, forty, and beyond. This crack was as tall as a multistory apartment building. The danger rained from above. First one stone, then another, small ones, big ones.

"Rocks!" the guys above would scream.

Larry and Brian crouched as best they could. More rocks were dislodged by the ropes creaking along the walls of the crack. Larry and Brian had their hardhats, but the clatter of the rocks, some of them small boulders, was terrifying. One strategic hit could be catastrophic. Larry and Brian started to communicate with Peter far below them. They hollered at him that they were coming, and told him to protect himself from the falling rocks. From Peter's end came a few murmurs of confirmation, and eventually silence. They had no idea what his condition would be when they reached him.

As they gained audible contact with him, the two rangers lost voice and radio communication with their colleagues above. About forty feet down was a narrow twist, an angle that apparently was blocking the radio contact. Now began a discussion about what to do next. Larry and Brian had no idea what was being planned up top. The isolation was frightening. They waited.

Larry Katahira, a Big Island native from Hilo, never set out to join the Park Service. He had wanted to be a teacher, but the jobs weren't there when he finished college. Volcanoes National Park did have openings, and Larry saw a chance to further his interest in biology and science. Now, five years later, he was comfortable in his career. But at this moment, swaying inside the earth, he was worried. He could see from the jagged rocks along the walls that Peter would have careened from one protrusion to the next on his fall. That's why he was still alive. A straight drop would have killed him. It also meant, however, that he must be badly cut up.

A voice came again from above. It was Gary Jones, from the nearby Kīlauea Military Camp. He had descended in the crack to a spot where he could communicate with the team above and also with the rescuers below. Now resumed the painstaking drop, stop, lurch, stop, as Larry and Brian were lowered. The ropes were played out when they finally saw Peter. He was at least 130 feet down, crumpled on a shelf that looked to be a flat-sided boulder that had wedged in the crack. The rescuers could stand on the shelf, but a step in almost any direction would send them plunging into a black abyss. It was almost miraculous that Peter had landed there.

He was lucky to hit the ledge, Larry thought, and luckier still that he hadn't moved around and toppled over the sides. Had he continued to fall, he would never have been found.

The rangers' headlamps revealed Peter's shredded, bloody clothes and skin. He was prone and barely able to speak. The two rescuers assessed his ability to be moved.

"Peter! Peter!" they yelled at him.

He was not communicative. He periodically fainted as they spoke to him. They needed to get him out of there soon. A litter, they saw, would not fit through the narrower passages of the crack. He would have to endure a harness. Peter was too weak to help himself into the harness. He would look at them for a while and then close his eyes. When they grabbed his arm, or gently moved his head, he yelled out in pain. They continued yelling in an effort to pull him from his stupor.

"Peter! Peter!"

Getting him into the harness was slow going. They fashioned some webbing into a seat, but Peter didn't have the strength to hold onto the ropes with his hands. He couldn't keep his body erect or his head up. The rangers saw that it would be up to them to keep him vertical, to keep his head from knocking into the walls. Suspended in the harness, Peter moaned in pain. Larry and Brian signaled to Gary that it was time to ascend. The three ropes inched upward, each pulling one man, with Brian just above the other two where the passage was not wide enough for all three to ascend together. Except where they were forced into single file, Larry stayed as close as he could to Peter to keep him from swaying into the walls, all the while terrified that a small earthquake might shift the boulders and trap all three of them. Ten feet, then a pause. If everything was okay, the rangers yelled "Pull!" Ten more feet, and a pause. It was agonizing to see Peter in so much pain, alternately hollering and passing out. Seeing his eyes closed worried the rangers, but they had no other options. They just needed to get out. With the ropes straining against the walls, rocks rattled down onto the trio.

"Rocks!" came the call from above.

The rangers leaned in to protect Peter and ducked their own heads. The ministorm bounced off their hardhats.

"Pull," they yelled.

They squinted up at the blackness. Nothing moved. They yelled again. The ropes were still. Now Larry and Brian saw the problem. A boulder had shifted and pinned the ropes beneath it. The pulling from above was only straining the rope more.

"Stop!" they screamed upward.

Any more tension on the stuck ropes could mean disaster. They were good ropes, but with enough strain they might snap, Larry thought.

Up top, the team waited for a signal from the crack. Brian managed to maneuver himself to the troublesome boulder. He dislodged it and the ropes swung free again. Again they inched up, slicing through an eternity of darkness, Peter mostly unconscious. Finally, light began to filter down. The lanterns that washed the rescue scene were reflecting down into the crack. Relief swept Larry and Brian, but the ordeal was not over.

Around the crack the mood was somber as the rescuers took turns pulling at the dead weight. Those taking a break would huddle together against the night air. Jack Jeffrey was paired with Jim Jacobi to haul on a rope. Jack was filled with remorse about Peter's accident, beating himself up about what he could have done differently to keep his colleague safe. Now he saw something that terrified him even more. Down where the rope was straining over the rocks, its fibers were separating, pulled apart as if it had been cut but not quite severed. This was no small cut, but a good-sized break where sharp lava had sliced the fibers. Peter was on the other end of this rope. Horrified, Jack and Jim leaned into the crack and grabbed the rope below the cut to relieve the strain. They hauled it up and averted crisis. But no one had any way of knowing whether there were more breaks in the ropes, or if one would snap while being dragged across the unforgiving rock.

The tension gave way to tentative relief when Peter's head finally appeared in the shadowy glare of the lanterns. His head was down. They couldn't see his face. Jacobi and Jeffrey pulled him by his jacket and shoulders and saw that he was conscious. They lifted him up and helped to stretch him out on a litter. Jack heard a murmur from Peter.

"Thanks."

His pain was clear to all. Mike thought Peter looked as if someone had taken a razor to him. He was sliced all over, covered in dirt and dried blood. Laurie, who had arrived after receiving word that he had been found, moved to his side. She peered anxiously into his face, not knowing what to expect. Like gems in the dark of a mine shaft, his blue eyes shone behind the caked dirt and blood.

"Hi, Pal," she said, patting his arm. "You're going to be okay."

He looked at her. "I know, Pal," he replied.

The team positioned Peter so that his spine was straight. A broken back was not beyond the realm of possibility. Jack gently cradled Peter's head in his hands. His fingers felt something squishy, wet, and studded with bits of rock. Jack was stunned.

Oh my god, what am I feeling here? he thought.

He slid his hands out. They were covered with blood. Peter had suffered a deep gash. But when they shined a light on his scraped up face, he managed the slimmest of smiles.

"You made it, Peter," someone said.

They reassured him he'd be fine, although they were far from confident. They were frightened for him. They still had to hike him out to the ambulance that would carry him to the hospital in Hilo. They took turns, four at a time, carrying the litter through the darkness, navigating the treacherously thick ferns to the open lava flow. Forty-five minutes later, they reached the road where the ambulance waited. It wasn't until Peter was loaded into the emergency vehicle and headed out of the park that the group relaxed. Emotions that had been buried by the tense effort of the rescue now were unleashed. Hugging, crying, clapping each other on the back, they were overwhelmed and exhausted. It was well after midnight.

Peter survived with his back intact. He had broken his collarbone, sternum, tailbone, and two vertebrae. He suffered a deep scalp cut. His skin was peeled back in places as if he had been burned. He spent several weeks recovering, both in Volcano and at his parents'

home in Colorado. Then he returned to his bird work. In the field, especially when plowing through ferns, he was careful to keep an eye on the ground.

Peter Paton moved back to the U.S. mainland after four years in Hawai'i. He teaches ornithology and conservation biology at the University of Rhode Island. Mike Scott became the director of the Condor Research Center in California, and later a research scientist for the U.S. Geological Survey and a professor at the University of Idaho. Larry Katahira became resource manager at Volcanoes National Park. Laurie MacIvor and Peter have remained friends through their separate marriages and careers. Laurie now teaches children in her home state of Oklahoma.

Peter Paton with spotted owl, 1986. Photo courtesy of Peter Paton.

First Ride of the Day

It was a strange, shaking feeling—like a dog chomping its teeth into a steak. The image vaguely flashed through Mike Coots's mind as the sensation overtook his lower body. It wasn't painful, just a remote feeling of shaking, jiggling, rattling. The way a dog would shake its head, back and forth. Before Mike had time to fully form the thought, however, the truth of the moment pierced his mind. Of course there was no dog in these waves off the shores of Kaua'i. It was a shark. And the meat was his own legs.

He turned to look over his shoulder, his arms clutching the red bodyboard he had been kicking into a wave that promised his first ride this morning. The urgency of catching the wave now melted away as his eyes registered the sight before him: a wide swath of gray—a mass that was not the length of the attacking fish's body, but the width of its face, accented by rows of serrated, furiously engaged teeth. For the longest fraction of a second, the eighteen-year-old surfer stared.

◇◇◇

Even by the rural standards of Kauaʻi, the west shore of this Hawaiian island was a remote place. It ran to the end of the road that encircled most of the island and bookended the famous Nā Pali Coast, a stretch of rugged cliffs accessible only by hiking trail or boat. Along the west side, white sand beaches unfolded across miles of undulating dunes. Kauaʻi earned its nickname, the Garden Isle, for its lush vegetation and forested mountains, including some of the wettest spots on earth, but here on the west side it was drier, with long stretches of unshaded beach. The Barking Sands Pacific Missile Range was on this shore, and the military allowed access through its gates to coveted surf spots. It was one of Mike's favorite bodyboarding locales. The waves weren't as gigantic as at Jaws, the monster break over on Maui where they towered so high that surfers had to be towed into position on Jet Skis, nor as fierce as at Oʻahu's famous North Shore, a Holy Grail of surfing and home of the deadly Banzai Pipeline. But Kauaʻi's west shore was known for its reliable waves that sometimes climbed to thirty feet and otherwise offered up plenty of rough-and-tumble training. With practice sites like this, Kauaʻi had spawned some of the world's most accomplished surfers and bodyboarders.

Mike lived several miles from Barking Sands in the town of Kalāheo with his surfing coach, Robert Sato, and bodyboard teammates. On this morning, Mike, teammate Kyle Maligro, and Sato were up at 5:30, excited about hitting the waves at Majors Bay up on the west side. The radio surf report on the previous night had brought the news they were waiting to hear: an early winter swell was on the way. That meant big waves, manna to Mike and his buddies who trained every day for bodyboard competitions. They eagerly awaited these seasonal swells.

Mike was especially anticipatory this morning. Growing up in Hawai'i, he had spent much of his life in the water, a bodyboard fanatic from a young age. His mind drifted to the beach as he waited for his teachers to release the class each day. Then he'd head off to the ocean and slip down the waves, one after another, until daylight was fading and his parents came to take him home. Ocean sports were his life, as important as eating and sleeping. When he was sixteen, his parents moved the family to New Zealand, where he won the national bodyboarding championship. By then, the tall, lean towhead knew he wanted to surf professionally. New Zealand was okay, but Mike pleaded to return to the idyllic conditions in Hawai'i, where he could pursue his surfing dreams. The family moved back for his senior year in high school.

In the fall of 1997, he was a new member of the Kaua'i Classic Team, coached by Sato, a videographer who also ran a foundation teaching young people photography and film production. Sato always had members of his bodyboard team living in his house, which simplified their surf-intensive daily routines. They'd rise in the morning, wolf down breakfast, and then head to the water. Sato would shoot video of them surfing, and when they weren't riding waves, they were watching the footage to improve their technique, or producing their own minivideos.

Aside from their surfing passion, the boys shared another bond: all were devout Christians. Mike had been surprised when he returned from New Zealand to learn that several friends had been "saved." He was skeptical at first, but when he began to tag along with them to church, he could see the appeal. An honor student from a close family, Mike was an easygoing kid with a ready grin, not into drugs or partying. His life was surfing, and he was good enough to place first in his age category on the Kaua'i circuit. But he also started to believe that he could improve his life by living the Christian way. He had long admired Sato's Christian surf team, which was earning a reputation in competitions both in Hawai'i and elsewhere. When he graduated from high school that summer, Mike moved in with them.

The team monitored daily ocean conditions around the island. On October 28, 1997, it looked like the best waves would be at Majors, and so, soon after first light, Mike and Kyle tossed their body-boards into Bob's four-wheeler and jumped in.

Kyle was twenty-seven and already had earned his stripes on the professional bodyboarding circuit. Along the way he relinquished the destructive behaviors of his youth for Christianity. Now he and Mike both were eager students under Bob's video production tutelage. Kyle thought that Mike was one of the mellowest guys he'd ever known, unflappable in any situation.

The sun was coming up over the rolling dunes of Majors beach. As Bob's four-wheeler bumped over the sand around 7 A.M., the trio could see several other surfers already heading into the ocean. The day was a little bit overcast and there was a strange smell in the air, almost like something rotten, Mike thought. He didn't dwell on it. He couldn't wait to jump in.

Bob wandered up the beach with his video camera, and Kyle and Mike paddled to the break, about one hundred yards out, joining the others already in position. The water, Kyle thought, was on the murky side. The surfers knew that sharks tended to be more prevalent when the water was cloudy, but the condition wasn't uncommon and certainly not something they dwelled on. This looked to be the start of a great day.

Soon everyone was catching waves, except Mike. He was impatient after ten minutes. He was the only one who hadn't caught a ride. Then at the tail end of a set, an inviting wave came his way. Alongside another surfer who was just a few feet from him, Mike kicked into position.

Kyle already had been pounded by a big wave and had paddled back out in time to snag another one that Mike missed. Kyle rode it a long way, almost to the beach and far from his friend. It took him awhile to get back to where he could see the other surfers clearly enough to notice that a handful of them were paddling toward shore. It looked fairly normal, no one splashing or yelling. They're moving closer for a better position, Kyle thought. He saw Mike near the others. Something was red at the back of his leg, probably his shorts or his jersey, or maybe I'm seeing things, Kyle thought, unfazed. As he got closer, he heard a panicky shout from the beach.

"SHARK!"

Sharks were well known in Hawai'i's waters. Attacks on humans were not frequent, but sightings of the big, shadowy forms gliding beneath the waves were not at all rare. Among the species seen in nearshore waters was the tiger shark. Because it prowled mostly at dusk or at night, it was spotted less frequently than other reef sharks, but was probably the most dangerous shark in these close waters and was the largest regular predator on the reef. With its dark stripes and wide, blunt head, a tiger was unmistakable. Its large mouth suited to gobbling hefty prey, it often dined on sea turtles or porpoises and scavenged reef areas for wounded fish. The tiger was distinguished by its serrated teeth, multiple rows of chompers arrayed like so many miniature saws for gnawing through bones or tough skin. The tiger tended to measure in the ten- to fourteen-foot range. Some were as long as sixteen feet.

Mike Coots had experienced one previous run-in with a shark. Out spearfishing with friends at the age of twelve, he was holding a rope attached to a floating buoy that held their catch. A reef shark appeared suddenly below him, attracted by the dead fish. Mike immediately released the rope and scrambled ashore with his companions. He watched as the shark grabbed the buoy and fish, jerking the whole apparatus beneath the water with a cavalier chomp. It was a sight to remember, but not one that deterred Mike from entering the ocean.

Now Mike stopped his forward motion, his body and head turning to the right where the broad gray face, maybe two feet wide, broke the surface of the water. Swiveling to his attacker, Mike saw the blunt, squarish nose. A tiger shark. It hadn't grabbed his board, but had a firm grip on his legs, which were dangling behind. It was shaking him like a child fighting for his teddy bear. The terrifying maw opened for another bite. Mike quickly slid off his board, holding it to his left side. He was looking down at the shark's head, his only physical sensation a strong pressure, as if something was sitting on his lower body. There was no pain. It was just creepy having this huge thing clamped onto him. He had to get it away from him. He felt his hands going around the shark's nose as he yanked his legs, trying to extract them from the big teeth. The shark clamped down tighter. Mike bent back, looking into the shark's face and trying to push off with his legs. He shot his right hand forward, close to the shark's mouth, in an effort to grab his ensnared leg. A razor-sharp tooth sliced his finger. Mike's left hand came around, in a swift and determined fist. With a whack, it made contact with the shark's face. The thick skin was solid, hard, unmoving. His left hook pummeled the face again, fast and hard and injected with all of Mike's strength. The struggle was over as suddenly as it started. The shark simply let go and slid beneath the water.

Mike slithered back onto his board and looked over at the other surfer, who sat wordless, his eyes huge.

"Shark!" Mike screamed. "Go in!"

The surfer turned and hightailed it toward shore. Mike also turned toward the beach. Still not registering physical pain, he tucked his board under his chest, and with his arms instinctively starting to rotate, he propelled himself forward. When his right hand came around he noticed his finger for the first time. He had never seen so much blood. The finger looked almost severed, the bone visible beneath a deep skin flap that peeled back. It was the most disgusting thing he had ever seen. Revulsed and afraid, Mike paddled urgently. He knew he had to get to shore fast. Something, however, was up with his right leg. He wasn't sure how it came to him, but he became aware that he was feeling a strange pulsation, an involuntary vibration. From the back of his mind the thought crept: it was back, grabbing him again. The gray beast had resurfaced and was here to finish him off.

Fully expecting to see the shark reattached to his legs, he turned to look. There was no shark. Neither was there cause for relief. What he saw was stunning. His right foot was gone. His leg was pulsing and squirting blood, like a gory Halloween movie scene. Mike's heart sank. He had no foot. It was an unfathomable, grotesque sight, and it terrified him. A wave was standing up behind him, the familiar arc of liquid color that shimmered like wind on a glassy wall, swelling and climbing until its power cascaded into rumbling foam. More from instinct than calculation, Mike whipped into position, caught the wave, and rode it to shore.

As soon as he heard the warning call from the beach, Kyle knew. That red on Mike's leg. A shark. How could he help his friend? He paddled toward Mike. He got close enough to see that he was hurt, but looking surprisingly strong. No yelling or panic—just calm, mellow Mike. He'd make it to shore, Kyle thought. He said a prayer for guidance. What should he do? He caught a wave to the beach, just before Mike caught the one that would carry him in. Mike landed on the sand and instinctively stood up to run from the water's edge. He toppled over instantly. Kyle and a few others gathered around him. Bob was far up the beach, unaware that anything was wrong. Covered in blood and sand, Mike rolled over. Kyle was leaning over him, pulling him higher on the beach. Mike could feel his heart pounding.

Oh my god, I'm going to die, he thought.

But to Kyle, Mike looked amazingly calm. He wasn't talking, crying, or freaking out. The sight of him, however, shocked Kyle. There was the bloody, midcalf stump on his right leg, but equally horrifying was the condition of his left. It was spurting blood from deep gouges where the shark had bitten above Mike's fin. Kyle put his hand on Mike's left leg.

"Lord, help us right now," he said. "Be with Mike. Give him strength and comfort him. Show us what we should do. In Jesus' name."

Then he heard Mike's voice.

"Lord, I'm trusting you are with us, and trust that you give me strength right now. Amen."

Kyle was astonished. How could Mike pray so peacefully, with no visible anger or panic? He had one leg missing and the other chewed up. It was crazy that he showed no fear. Kyle didn't pause to reflect. He found himself grabbing the rubbery leash from a boogie board on the sand, a crucial accessory that kept the board attached to a surfer's ankle in the water. Instinctively, Kyle wrapped it around Mike's severed leg just above the kneecap and tied it off tightly, a tourniquet. He'd never done anything like this before, but something told him to take this lifesaving action.

With Kyle's prayer, Mike felt suddenly relaxed, as calm as he'd ever been. He heard his friend telling him not to worry, that everything would be all right.

"God, please help Mike and make it stop bleeding," he heard Kyle say.

He closed his eyes. When he opened them a truck was there waiting for him.

Keith Karasic, a forty-two-year-old professional photographer, was like countless Hawai'i residents who arranged his work life so that surfing could be part of his daily routine. This day was no exception. He loaded three surfboards into his tan Chevy pickup and drove down to Majors. In the parking area at the edge of the sand he ran into a couple of friends and they sat chatting as they evaluated the water conditions. They saw a flurry in the water where everyone was surfing. The surfers were all paddling in. To Keith, it looked humorous at first, like the Keystone Cops all running around. Were they scrambling for a set? Then he noticed they were heading to the beach. A shark, he figured. They probably saw one lurking out there and got spooked, but none of them looked to be in trouble. As they reached the sand, a tall youth rose out of the water and promptly collapsed on the beach. Keith's first thought was that he was missing a fin. Then the truth jolted him. The guy was missing a foot! Keith immediately thought of calling 911 on his cellular phone. Just as quickly, he began calculating. This guy needed a ride to the hospital. Keith could probably get him there faster than an ambulance that would have to figure out where they were and then negotiate the sand to get down here. He turned the key in his ignition and beelined to Mike and Kyle 150 yards away on the sand.

There was no discussion as Keith pulled up parallel to the ocean and announced he would ferry Mike to the hospital. The others simply picked him up and set him on the hard truck bed. In the intensity of the moment, it didn't occur to Keith to throw out his surfboards or look for towels, or for that matter to close the lift gate. He noticed the leash around Mike's leg and assumed he had gotten tangled in it. He was bleeding profusely. The image that came to Keith was that of a big, speared fish being trucked to market. Mike was helping to scoot himself back, and apologizing to Keith for the inconvenience. Keith leaped back into the cab, and before Kyle could climb aboard to be with his friend, he took off. Keith concentrated on crossing the sand carefully so that he didn't get stuck or, worse, drop Mike out the open tailgate.

When he reached the parking area where he had watched Mike come out of the water, he called 911. He asked for an ambulance and said he would meet it enroute to Kaua'i Veterans Memorial Hospital, about seven miles from the military base. To save time, Keith headed to a side gate on the base instead of the main gate, where visitors to the beach were supposed to enter. Once on the two-lane main road, he accelerated. He flew by morning commuters, honking and flashing his lights, checking repeatedly to make sure Mike was secure in the back. He prayed Mike wouldn't pass out. He stuck his head out the window, yelling at motorists to get out of his way. Accustomed to the unfailingly courteous mores of Hawai'i's roadways, they didn't respond to his aggressive behavior. After he went around them, he could see in his rearview mirror that the truck bed awash in blood, not to mention the blood spraying out the back, must have shocked them. Some of the cars veered violently to the side of the road. Mike, too, saw the motorists' looks of horror. He didn't want to look at the blood either. He was shaking and cold, then alternately hot. Jostled next to Keith's surfboards, he focused intently on the light cotton covering over the one nearest him. He fingered the fabric, trying to keep his eyes away from his leg or his right hand. Concentrating on the fabric helped him stay calm. He reassured himself that everything would be okay.

After the longest five minutes of his life, Keith roared up to the hospital. Where was everybody? He ran inside. He learned the ambulance had been dispatched, but had entered the base through the main gate and missed him on the road. Keith grabbed someone with a gurney. He went out as Mike, indomitable, was shimmying his way to the edge of the lift gate. He was apologizing to everyone for the trouble and especially for getting sand all over. Keith reached for him with both arms and picked him up. He couldn't help being intensely aware of Mike's severed leg, cradled for that second in the crook of his arm. It was so cleanly cut that it didn't seem possible it was the remnant of a savage attack.

Fifteen minutes ago, there was a foot here, Keith thought as he whisked Mike onto the gurney.

Inside the hospital, Mike became hazy. He passed out as emergency workers treated him, and woke up in an ambulance racing to a hospital on the other side of the island where he would undergo surgery. The paramedic was talking to him, telling him he knew Mike's stepfather, who was also a paramedic. Now for the first time, Mike had intense pain in his leg. He was in a fog. He lost consciousness again.

A few days later, Mike's lost fin washed up on the beach, the rubber shredded and imprinted with jagged teeth marks. No doubt the fin had saved his left foot, along with the shark's inability to chomp all the way down on both legs at once.

Mike's leg surgery was successful. His left ankle was stitched up. He underwent nerve surgery on his hand. He was fitted with a prosthesis that attached below the knee. He walked with crutches in a week, and soon didn't need them. From his friends to his medical team, there wasn't anyone who wasn't impressed with the young man's composure and determination. Two months after the attack, he was back in the water. He felt his bodyboarding skills actually improved without the right foot. Or maybe he was just trying harder. He competed some, and placed. Soon, however, he was off to college and was busy with other activities, still surfing but mostly working on his goal to become a professional photographer. It wasn't that Mike never felt down about being unable to run and hike like he once did. But he told himself that the shark attack was just something that happened to him, that he was lucky to have his life and a caring family. He didn't see a half-empty glass. He felt fortunate for all the things he could still do. Before long he had a waterproof prosthesis and mastered a new challenge: regular stand-up surfing. He looked forward to getting still another leg that would allow him to run. He visited schools occasionally and advised the kids to look on the positive side of life, not to let setbacks drag them down. When another Kaua'i teenager lost his leg to a shark five years later, Mike Coots went to the hospital to reassure the boy's family. He told them not to worry, that everything would be okay.

After a stint at community college, a TV internship, and an editing job with a foundation, Mike Coots was accepted and enrolled at the Brooks Institute of Photography. He continues to be an avid surfer. Kyle Maligro moved to California and started a clothing business. He is an elder with a Christian church. Keith Karasic remained on Kaua'i, a professional photographer and surfer.

Mike Coots, Kaua'i, 2003

The Ledge

Considering the alternatives, this was a decent ledge, at least compared with what else the rocky shores of Nihoa Island had to offer. The scientists liked it because although it was only about six feet deep in actual working space, it hooked onto an expanded section of ledge farther back from the sea. There they could stack the gear they unloaded from their raft, and they didn't have to worry about waves surging up and drenching everything. Gene Kridler always had pretty good luck getting on and off this ledge. On his periodic visits, he and his team would conduct research for a few days, camping out on the uninhabited island, then drop back down from the ledge and be on their way. For the most part, their sporadic comings and goings had become a smooth enough routine at this remote place. Until, that is, the day when the ocean decided to give Gene a hard time, a lesson in humility, or maybe just a little reminder about where the real power lay.

Perhaps the island just wasn't meant to be roamed by two-legged mammals. The remains of rock temples and terraces on Nihoa attested to the long-ago presence of Polynesians who had sailed from

Tahiti to Nihoa and its neighbor, Necker Island. But eventually they left. Maybe Gene had become too confident in his routine. He would never know why, but now the waters that guarded the island were going to show him who was boss.

Nihoa was little more than an oversized rock poking up from the Pacific waters. Like other islands in the Hawaiian archipelago, it was the remnant of a volcano that had erupted here ages ago and had long since cooled and slid back to the sea. The bit of leftover cone that constituted Nihoa was one in a string of land smudges north of the main Hawaiian island chain, collectively called the Northwest Hawaiian Islands. The easternmost was Nihoa, closest to the better-known, populated islands of Hawai'i, but still separated from them by more than one hundred miles of rugged sea. On one side of the 146-acre Nihoa were sheer cliffs. On the other side were the small rock shelves that jutted above sea level. There wasn't a beach anywhere. So it was always a challenge for Gene Kridler and his crew to get ashore.

Gene was manager of the Hawaiian Islands National Wildlife Refuge for the federal Fish and Wildlife Service. Part of his job was to make periodic visits to Nihoa and the other islands, reefs, and atolls in the eight-hundred-mile-long Northwest refuge. It was no simple feat to visit these islands. The refuge, which extended almost to Midway Atoll, wasn't the kind of place that tourists would or could go. There wasn't a scrap of infrastructure or transportation. To get there meant navigating waters that typically were traversed only by the sturdiest fishing boats and definitely not for the weak of stomach. Gene and his teams usually hitched a ride from Honolulu with a Coast Guard boat that was enroute to its outpost in the Northwest Islands. That meant an overnight voyage just to reach Nihoa.

Visiting the refuge was well worth the effort. Biologists and wildlife experts considered it a special experience just to see the rare species that proliferated in this pristine environment. At least seventy-two species of unique insects were documented on Nihoa alone. Blizzards of birds and colonies of rare green turtles and monk seals basked under the crisp blue sky. The surrounding waters and reefs boasted a riot of fish in a profusion long since disappeared around the major Hawaiian islands. Gene's role was to generally keep tabs on the wildlife here. It often entailed surveying different species.

Landing on Nihoa was a tricky business. Gene's team used a motorized rubber raft because the waves that battered the island's rock face prevented the Coast Guard or other ships from getting in close. The challenge of the waves demanded an intricately timed unloading process. The biologists would let the ocean swell lift their raft as close to the height of the ledge as possible. They had a few strategic seconds to leap from the raft to the shelf and, with subsequent swells, to toss gear from the boat to those ashore. The water would recede, taking the boat down a few feet or as much as twenty feet, depending on the size of the swells. The team waited for the water to rise again before repeating the process to send more gear over. It was grueling work. They had to scurry to avoid the waves that washed over the ledge. Once the gear was unloaded, they would rope it up about forty feet higher, to the next flat place, and climb up a small trail to their camping spot. One errant throw could vanquish a duffel bag. One misstep on the slippery ledge could plunge a crew member into roiling surf and against the treacherous rocks. Gene had seen many hair-raising landings in the refuge. The waves sometimes were so wild that he and his colleagues had to leap into as much as twenty feet of air, like circus performers, just to get back down to the bobbing raft. Gene joked that he had nearly made his wife a widow many times with the unheralded perils of his job.

But the challenges never deterred Gene Kridler, a Midwesterner and World War II veteran who had earned college degrees in forestry and wildlife management. He was dedicated to the preservation of these islands. In 1964, he became the first-ever manager of the refuge, and later would become wildlife administrator for the whole U.S. Pacific region, a post he held until he retired in 1980. Kridler was especially interested in species that were in danger of extinction—an all-too-common feature in Hawai'i, which was known as the endangered species capital of the world. The islands' geographical isolation, as well as their diverse geography, had evolved a huge variety of plants and animals found nowhere else, with levels of endemic species unmatched anywhere in the world. But these species had suffered a staggering decline following human contact. Already half of the birds were extinct, and many more were in trouble, not to mention the green sea turtles, monk seals, and other marine, mammal, and plant species on the endangered species list. The major Hawaiian islands had suffered the most, as grazing, urban development, alien species, and pollution took a toll on delicate ecosystems. Human contact, including military activity and years of shipwrecks, to a much lesser degree had left its imprint on the northwest islands. Kridler had nightmares about rats escaping from wrecked ships and wreaking untold damage on the islands' vulnerable bird populations.

It was the proliferation of unique birds that prompted President Theodore Roosevelt to bestow the protected refuge status on the

Northwest Hawaiian Islands in 1909. The refuge harbored more than fourteen million sea birds, some of the greatest nesting colonies in the world. Nihoa was home to two species found nowhere else, the grayish brown Nihoa millerbird and the small, yellow Nihoa finch. Gene took stunning photographs of the wildlife and developed plans for managing the refuge for preservation. He wrote extensive reports and publications about the place for the government. He was hoping that the work he did might allow his grandchildren someday to see the wonders he had witnessed.

Gene conducted semiannual inspection trips to the refuge throughout most of the 1960s, typically with a small crew of researchers and biologists in tow. On one particular trip he headed a team of four wildlife experts, from the University of Hawai'i, the state government, and the U.S. Fish and Wildlife Service. Ernie Kosaka, a wildlife biologist for the state of Hawai'i, had volunteered for this trip and was excited to be returning to the refuge to see its unique wildlife. It was a rare opportunity, even for a researcher, to visit these islands. On this trip, the primary mission was to assess the condition of the Nihoa finch and millerbird and check on wildlife farther up the chain.

The Coast Guard didn't have a boat going to the northwest islands at this time, so the researchers hitched a ride on a small ship from the Bureau of Commercial Fisheries, a sister agency at the time to the Fish and Wildlife Service. The group packed camping gear and food they would need as they spent two or three days on different islands and atolls. The ship would drop them at each location and return to pick them up.

Gene usually traveled light—eschewing even a tent because it was too bulky—but he had extra gear on this trip. One of his tasks was to erect a sign on Nihoa, identifying this as the beginning point of the Hawai'i National Wildlife Refuge. That meant he had to lug not only the sign and two large wooden posts, but also cement to anchor it to the ground and withstand the storms.

The seas were particularly foul as the familiar outline of Nihoa, two small peaks spanned by a low-slung saddle, came into view that morning. The group knew that sometimes it just wasn't safe for the raft to go in. They discussed whether this was one of those times, but ultimately decided they could make it. As they neared the shore, they saw that the waves were pounding violently against the cliffs. The usual method of tossing gear onto the ledge wasn't going to work today. The raft wouldn't be able to get in close enough to the ledge to offload the big haul they were carrying. They came up with an alternative. The raft anchored at a safe distance from shore. They rigged up a rope system, using a water-tight container the size of a barrel. The container was roped to the raft on one side, and also to a length of rope that extended to the shore. They loaded gear into the container, then tossed it into the surf and pulled it up to the ledge using the rope. They unloaded it and sent it back out to the raft, then hauled it back to shore to repeat the process.

Gene and Ernie, with their colleague Andy Berger, positioned themselves on the ledge to receive the loads. As the large Coast Guard ship watched from a distance, they began hauling the gear ashore. As usual, Gene took the forward, most dangerous post. He always held the view that as the one in charge, he should assume the most risk. He sent the barrel back dozens of times for more loads as the day wore on. The wind picked up, and now the waves were even rougher, crashing as high as fifteen feet when they smashed into the ledge. The men were getting soaked.

Finally, they were down to the last few loads. The barrel was ready to go back out to the raft for another refill. Ernie and Andy were stacking gear at the back of the ledge and Gene was working the rope by the lip of the shelf when a voracious wave rose up over the edge like a lunging tiger. Gene was engulfed and blasted off his feet. He clutched at the rock, grabbing frantically for anything he could put his hands on. His fingers got only air. The wave catapulted him over the edge of the shelf. Ahead of him, the barrel was whooshed seaward. Inexplicably, the rope attached to it became tangled around Gene's ankle as he toppled over. He went flying after the barrel. But his wrist was looped into the rope leading to shore. Ernie had the other end of that rope. He had been holding it slack, and now looked up to see his colleague disappear over the side, the rope snaking after him. Adrenaline shot through Ernie.

Oh god, this can't be happening, he thought.

The waves, he knew, were rough, but to see Gene swept away was shocking. He clutched the rope taut in both hands and hollered to Andy who was right behind him. Andy, older than Ernie and not as strong, grabbed onto the rope too. It strained with Gene's weight dangling over the side.

Gene was plunged into the swirling sea, banged like a loose shutter against the rock face. He was spread-eagled, his foot pulled out to sea with the barrel and his wrist yanked back to the ledge by his colleagues while the water knocked him around. With his free leg, Gene tried to kick off the rock wall to keep from getting smashed against it. He was only partly successful. The water spun him around and pounded him against the face again. The rocks scraped and cut his flesh. He tried to pull himself up by the rope on his wrist but the receding wave was too strong. It dragged the retreating barrel seaward, and yanked Gene after it. The water surged and threw him to the rocks again. Gene knew that if he let the rope go from his wrist, he would be pulled under, left to the mercy of the watery maelstrom. He hung on.

Up top, Ernie and Andy dragged at the rope with all their strength, pitting their weight against the force of the water that was accustomed to taking no prisoners. It now had Gene dangling in the trough of a breaking wave. Ernie's mind flashed to the stories of 'opihi pickers who were swept out to sea along the rocky Hawaiian coastlines where they collected the edible snails. The cap-shelled 'opihi was able to withstand the heavy surges and pounding waves by clinging to the rocks with a suction-like foot. Unlike Gene and the 'opihi pickers, the limpets could burrow into shallow depressions in the rock, protecting themselves from rough waters at high tide and exposure at low tide. There was no such protection for the pickers who plucked them from the rocks. Some were lost to the sea forever. Ernie knew that Gene was perilously close to going the same way. If he banged his head and was knocked out, that would be the end of him.

Ernie fiercely clung to the rope, bracing himself as best he could on the slippery surface. There was certainly the chance that his own footing would slip and send him down with Gene. But Ernie and Andy weren't about to let go. The ocean banged Gene into the rock again. Ernie felt a give in the rope. The next wave crashed and the water swirled up, carrying Gene with it. As his weight was buoyed, his two colleagues yanked furiously, helping Gene fight his way to the edge of the shelf. They pulled him against the force of the wave as it receded. Gene's hands came over the top of the ledge. He clutched the rocky surface. His colleagues lunged at him, grabbing him up before the water could take him out again. Gene crumpled onto the rock, battered but safe.

It had happened fast, but the ordeal seemed like a lifetime. The men were all exhausted. Gene could barely move. He was stiff and sore and cut up, but incredibly had suffered no broken bones. With the sea pounding even harder, the group waved off the raft. It would be smashed if it tried to come in and collect Gene. They signaled to the large ship to go on as well, and to return for them two days later as planned.

The men helped Gene up the trail, amazed at what had happened. By the next morning, Gene was so stiff that he needed help to get out of his sleeping bag and stand up. He hobbled around and helped as best he could with the new sign and the bird census, using his camera tripod as a crutch. Ernie wasn't surprised at Gene's grit. When Gene Kridler set out to do something, it took more than a little wave action to throw him off track.

The group finished their work and the Coast Guard returned and retrieved them for the voyage home. When Gene returned to his Honolulu home, his wife asked what on earth had happened that he had so many scratches and bruises. Gene didn't want to worry her.

"I fell down," he replied.

Gene Kridler retired from the U.S. Fish and Wildlife Service in 1980, with a string of honors to his name. He lives on the Olympic Peninsula in Washington. Ernie Kosaka left Hawai'i state employ and works for the Fish and Wildlife Service in Honolulu.

Gene Kridler with Laysan teal, Laysan, 1969. Photo courtesy of Gene Kridler.

From right, Gene Kridler, Ernie Kosaka, Andy Berger, and another researcher on Nihoa Island, 1967. Photo courtesy of Gene Kridler.

No Work on Sunday

Leo Ohai had promised his youngest daughter: no more working on Sundays. For a long time, he'd been working seven days a week. Either he'd be out on his fishing boat, hauling in nets of *akule,* or up in his plane looking for the next catch. He kept an apartment in Honolulu because that's where his fishing business was, and sometimes it was a good long while before he'd get back to his home on the neighboring island of Kaua'i. On the Friday after New Year's, 1967, Laole called him from Utah, where she was at college.

"What's your New Year's resolution, Dad?" Obviously she had something in mind.

"What do you want me to do?" he asked.

"Okay," she said. "No more fishing on Sunday. No working on Sunday."

Ohai had to agree. Fishing was his life, and hard work was all he knew. It was tough raising six kids, with several off to college (three more would come into his life in later years), if you didn't work hard. For years, he had had his own business, running as many as three fishing boats and selling millions of pounds of fish. His wholesale customers were steady—grocery stores and markets. Business was pretty good, but Laole was right. Fishing was in his blood, but it had gotten to be too much.

"Okay," he told Laole. "No more work on Sunday."

In truth, it was an easy promise to make at that particular moment. He had just caught a big school of fish and his crew was still unloading the haul. There was no need to go flying this weekend to scout more fishing spots, because the boat couldn't go out again anyway until it was unloaded. So he worked that Saturday, and on Sunday morning, he got together with a couple of his customers, as he often did, for breakfast at a favorite Chinese joint. But after eating, Leo said goodbye to them, got in his car, and drove straight to the airport. A week earlier, he had spotted a school of fish off the small island of Lāna'i. He had no thoughts of his daughter. He just wanted to check and see if those fish were still there.

Three of Ohai's five planes were at Honolulu Airport that day. He usually parked the others on Maui or Kaua'i, sometimes the Big Island. He always kept two or three in Honolulu for his own use and for pilots who helped him. They were all PA12 Supercruisers, single-engine three seaters, with the propeller on the nose and the wings stretching above the side doors, so the pilot had to duck his head under the wing to get in. Ohai had a lot of faith in this workhorse and swore by its reliability.

At the airport, he ran into a friend who spotted fish for him. This friend had a preference for a particular one of Leo's planes. He had just filled the fuel tank, but wasn't going up himself, so he urged Leo to take it. The one that Leo usually flew needed to be gassed up. Leo opted for the one that was ready to go, and lifted off.

There was a strong wind from the north, not great for flying, and small craft warnings were up. The ocean had been especially rough in recent days. Leo was unconcerned. He lived up to his reputation as a gutsy and confident pilot, at ease in flying conditions that other pilots wouldn't chance. In fact, people regularly called him to help find missing pilots. The Coast Guard knew him by name. There was that time his friend's pilot son, Robert Whittinghill, was reported missing on a flight out of Kaua'i. The weather was very bad, and it was dark by the time the report came in. The Coast Guard wasn't planning to search until morning. Leo, however, had a hunch about where the boy might have gone. A few weeks earlier, Leo had flown the teenager to the isolated island of Ni'ihau, across from Kaua'i, to collect lobsters. He warned the boy never to try the dangerous landing on Ni'ihau on his own. Now he had a feeling Bobby might have disregarded the warning. So despite a heavy gale, he had hopped into his own plane. He searched Ni'ihau, shining a dimestore flashlight out his plane window. Sure enough, there was the glint of an aircraft on the ground in the rainy night. The young pilot, with a friend, was stranded, uninjured, alongside his crashed plane.

Leo had not filed a flight plan that night, nor did he on this Sunday morning in 1967. He never did. But as always, he kept his radio on. As soon as he was airborne, he called the Honolulu tower to be sure the radio was working.

"Radio check, forty-three mike checking in. How do you read?" he said using his call sign.

"We read you loud and clear," the tower reported.

Leo rogered off. He didn't mention where he was headed. He climbed out of Honolulu, shedding the congestion of Hawai'i's only urban environment. He flew along the coast of Oʻahu to Hawaiʻi Kai, where he also wanted to check for fish. Then the little plane cleared Oʻahu and soared above 1,500 feet. Far below, whitecaps bounced atop the wind-whipped ocean. Flying over these stunning waters was always scenic, but Leo's mind was on that school of fish. He'd cruise east across the channel, fly alongside Molokaʻi, and then drop down over the small island of Lānaʻi, some seventy miles from Honolulu.

He was about a third of the way to Molokaʻi, out over the Kaiwi Channel, when he heard it: a loud bang, coming from the engine. Like a gunshot.

What the hell is going on here? Leo said to himself. He took a look at his propeller. It wasn't whirring at all. It was rotating ever so slowly. The finality of the image stabbed into Leo's mind. This was about as clear a choice as he'd ever have to make. He grabbed his radio.

"Forty-three mike mayday! Forty-three mike mayday! Forty-three mike mayday!"

◇◇◇

Leo Ohai never went to flying school. Not formally. The finer skills of piloting he learned mostly from his older brother Ben, who was the first to buy a plane. Leo was already in the fishing business, pursuing the life he had cherished since boyhood. His father, a farmer and fish and game warden, had ardently discouraged his fisherman dreams, expecting him to attend college on the mainland like his brothers. But there was no stopping Leo. He bought his first small fishing business while he was still in high school, and quickly made good money, so good that he was able to supplement his father's income and support his brothers away at school.

A few years later, in 1946, he added aerial fish-spotting to the business. Looking for fish from a plane was still a new idea, but it was highly efficient for fishermen who tracked large schools of fish. Leo had a friend who spotted for him. When Leo accompanied him or Ben, he picked up enough pointers to know that he could fly the contraption, too. Soon he had his own plane and was doing his own spotting. In a couple of hours, he could scout out promising bays and reefs and cover a distance that might take a fishing boat days to check out. He usually fished a near-shore mackerel called *akule,* which swam in schools that sometimes numbered more than one hundred thousand. From the air, the schools appeared as large shadows in the ocean. They could resemble underwater rocks, but a fish spotter could tell the difference. After finding a school, Leo would guide his boat to the location. His crew cast giant nets to corral the fish, and divers went into the water to "work" the nets, condensing the fish into smaller and smaller areas until they could be hauled into the boat, tens of thousands at a time.

◇◇◇

No question about it, Leo was going to have to ditch his plane in the channel. He had no idea what was wrong, wouldn't find out until later that his drive shaft most likely had broken. All he knew was that this was going to be a rough landing. The waves were huge. Leo was a good judge of distance, but this was iffy. Although he had no power, he still had control of the plane with the stick. Normally, the preferred landing would be into the wind for a slow approach, but in this case, that would plunge him right into the wave, where he would be an instant submarine. Aiming for the top of the crest, he faced the danger of hitting it with the plane's nose, and that would tip him right into the trough. The only viable prospect, although not exactly promising, was crosswind. In his countless hours in the cockpit, he'd never made a water landing. With his fixed-landing-gear aircraft, it would be very difficult in these rough waters. Leo decided he would make this one, and that's all there was to it.

He took off his seatbelt and glanced at the backseat. There was a life raft. Leo's friend who usually flew this plane had stowed it aboard because he was not a swimmer. A nylon rope was attached from the raft to an empty gallon container, intended to keep the raft from getting away before a downed pilot could inflate it. Leo didn't have time to think about that. Gripping his control stick, he watched the water. This was going to be a matter of luck. A monster wave was rolling toward him. He had no way to know whether it would crash on top of him or slip beneath him as he came in. The wave gathered itself into a crest. Leo dropped the tail wheel. He beelined for the water and dragged his tail wheel across the top of the wave. As gentle as a sea bird, the plane sat down right on top of that wave. It was the perfect landing. Not even a jolt or a bounce.

It was frankly astounding—for about a half second. Leo had no chance to congratulate himself before the wave broke and barreled him over. Blasted from the side, his plane tipped wing over wing. Now upside down in the cockpit, Leo kicked the door open. Water rushed in. He pushed himself out the door. A wave raked over him, pushing him under. He kicked his way up and toward the back of his plane. He stared at it, a bit confounded. For no reason, an odd thought popped into his mind: his raw fish. He had prepared himself his favorite snack, raw *akule*, and left it back in his refrigerator at home. He had forgotten to bring it, and the realization was just occurring to him now. Before he could focus on this lapse and wonder what in the world was causing him to have such a strange reflection, another thought knifed into his mind. What the devil was he doing out here? He had promised his daughter he wouldn't fly on Sunday. Maybe God was punishing him here in the middle of the Kaiwi Channel.

His daughter. God. The raw fish in his icebox. The raft.

He had to get that raft out of the plane! He dove through the submerging door and blindly groped in the upside-down plane. When his hand felt the raft, he yanked at it. It stuck. He pulled again, then came up for air without it. Diving down again, he realized that the nylon rope with the gallon container was tangled around the control stick. There was no way to get it unwound. He felt for the end of the rope. Maybe he could untie it from the raft. His fingers found a stubborn knot. He tried but couldn't undo it. He was out of air. He surfaced again. The knot was hopeless. He dove and yanked. The raft yielded and he pulled it outside the plane. He had the raft now, but it was still tethered to the stick inside the plane. He worked feverishly on the knot but it didn't look good. Something whacked him on the shoulder. The wing of the plane. The aircraft was going down. Now there was no choice. He had to let the raft go. He backed away from the plane. It was like watching a movie: The plane's nose dipped into the water and then the whole craft stood up, like a breaching whale frozen in a pose. It slipped quickly beneath the waves, its tail disappearing last. The plane was gone. Waves churned over the spot, giving no clue that anything had been there.

Leo looked up and saw an airliner circling. The pilot, flying the commercial shuttle between the islands, had heard his mayday call. But Leo was only a tiny speck. He knew the pilot couldn't see him. The jet turned and continued on toward Maui. Leo bobbed for a few minutes in the whitecap-flecked ocean, evaluating his situation. In this rough sea, without a raft or a flare. he would be virtually invisible to searchers. It was only midmorning. He was going to have to swim for it. It was hardly a devastating thought. He had no doubt that if he could see land, he could swim to it.

To say that Leo was a strong swimmer was like stating a fact of nature, that the tides rose and the trade winds blew across Hawai'i. Leo was as comfortable in the water as he was anyplace else. Tall, lanky, and strong at forty-four, he had practically grown up in the ocean. As a kid he fished and dove with his brothers almost every day. They'd spearfish after school and sell their catch, making the excellent wage of about a dollar a day, even in elementary school. Later, when he fished with large nets, Leo would spend entire nights in the water, free diving to work the nets. Nighttime fishing was part of the business, a way to take advantage of the window when the moon and tides were best for fishing. Leo had worked plenty of nets in his life. If there was one thing he knew, it was ocean currents.

The channel between Moloka'i and O'ahu measured twenty-two miles, but Leo believed it was a little less than that at its very narrowest point. He looked back toward Honolulu, figuring it was less than nine miles and the best option from the standpoint of distance. On the other hand, he would take a beating against the north wind and the enormous waves. Moloka'i was a longer swim but strategically looked like a better choice. The wind was blowing from O'ahu down to the smaller island, right toward Lā'au Point on the southwest corner of Moloka'i. He'd have the wind at his back if he headed that way and looked for a landing spot on Moloka'i's southern coast.

He struggled out of his pants, shirt, and shoes and got himself lined up. As a pilot he knew every geographical landmark on the islands. But he couldn't just swim straight to Moloka'i. He'd have to factor in the nasty current that whipped between Moloka'i and its small neighbor island, Lāna'i. If it captured him, he would be dragged on up to the northwest corner of the island—the opposite of what he wanted. He would have to be vigilant as he headed toward Lā'au Point, staying well clear of the point itself because that was where the current was strong. He'd have trouble if he tried to get ashore there. He figured he'd want to round the point and swim a few miles beyond it on the south shore to a harbor called Hale o Lono. He occasionally had landed his plane on a little airstrip there. There was a rock and cinder mining operation, and some of the workers probably would recognize him. Aside from Hale o Lono, his other landing prospects were mostly cliffs and forbidding rock, and with the swells this time of year, he'd get battered trying to come ashore any closer to Lā'au Point. For now, the wind would help him get to Moloka'i and then he could deal with the currents. Leo pointed himself to a spot between Moloka'i and Lāna'i and started stroking in ten-foot waves.

First one, then another small plane flew low, searching for him. They were close. He waved furiously, but each time they flew off, unable to see him in the choppy sea. The next time a plane appeared,

Leo took no comfort in its presence. He didn't even stop swimming. He had accepted his invisibility. Word, however, was spreading around the islands. When Leo's son Levon, a teacher, heard that his father had crashed, he had one thought. As long as Leo was not unconscious or seriously injured, there was no way that he would perish in the ocean. He would swim to safety. He could and would survive. Levon knew his dad's fortitude. Levon himself took a plane up to search for him. He could see nothing in the frothy whitecaps that were so choppy they resembled a dusting of snow on the ocean. Still, Levon never doubted his father would make it. Other people talked about the rough waters and questioned whether anyone could survive those conditions.

Well, thought Levon, *they don't know my dad.*

Down in the whitecaps, Leo was contending with not only the waves but an army of Portuguese man-of-wars, the purplish jellyfish with hanging tentacles. They attacked him en masse, wrapping around his neck, hanging down his shoulders, stinging his ears and body. They were everywhere. Leo couldn't fend them off, so he tried to keep going and not think about it until he got beyond them. There was nothing he could do except keep swimming, stroke after stroke, perpetual motion in steady determination.

He focused on the island ahead of him. Aiming to the south coast, he kept himself at an angle well offshore to avoid the current running north up the west side of the island. As he climbed up and over the waves, salt water splashed into his nose again and again. He hit on the idea of plugging his nostrils with little strips of rolled up cotton that he tore from his skivvies.

A few hours of methodical swimming brought him within two

miles of the Moloka'i coast. He kept his eye on the lighthouse at Lā'au Point. He would swim past it to Hale o Lono. But then the lighthouse was no longer where it was supposed to be. Instead of moving to his left as he swam past, it was crossing in front of him to the right. He was still stroking forward, but the current had caught him. It was pulling him exactly opposite of where he wanted to go, to the north of the island, where there would be no hope of coming ashore. He was powerless to fight the current that was flowing like whitewater rapids. The next thing he knew he had traveled almost the width of Moloka'i and was far north.

Leo was furious. He looked across the channel to O'ahu. If this was his fate, he decided, he would simply swim back. Daylight was fading, but he didn't care if it took him all night. He would swim across the channel and back to Honolulu. The water had flattened out and he didn't feel tired. He turned to carry out his new plan, but now a strange thing happened. The current seemed to stop, and then began flowing the opposite way. Before he could change his own course, he was moving south again, this time able to swim with the help of a gentle current. He was back on track for Hale o Lono Harbor.

He continued to stroke through the waves as the sun faded below the horizon. In the darkness, he heard a whooshing noise at his back. He glanced over his shoulder to see a large phosphorescent streak. It seemed to surf the wave behind him. A porpoise, maybe, he thought. Bioluminescence in the water was nothing new. Leo had often seen the tiny marine organisms that lit up when disturbed. In fact, Leo's arms were making phosphorescent streaks as he swam.

It dawned on him as he thought about the whooshing streak

behind him that this was not a porpoise, but a shark. These waters were filled with sharks, and in fact, it was somewhat surprising that he hadn't encountered any yet. Leo kept swimming. He'd been around sharks all his life and never had a problem. Hawaiian legend was filled with stories of sharks as ‘aumākua, or guardians, even as guides for navigators. Bam. Leo felt a whack at the side of his body. The shark was hitting him! It slammed along his side, scraping him with its rough skin, a sideswipe so powerful that its skin cut into Leo's flesh. Leo kept swimming. When he was young, his grand-mother, who spoke only Hawaiian, used to go out on the reef with food wrapped in ti leaves. She told Leo, who spent a lot of time fish-ing and talking with her, that she'd been feeding a shark all those times. The shark made another pass and scraped Leo again, not as hard this time, but painfully. Leo was now riled. He figured that fish just wanted him to know that it was in charge out here and could bite him any time. It had made its point. The shark turned and swam away, leaving Leo bleeding but still swimming single-mindedly.

Eventually he found himself all the way back to Lā‘au Point. The water was calmer now. The lighthouse was again moving left in front of him as he flowed along the coast. He was between Lāna‘i and Moloka‘i, heading to Hale o Lono, just where he wanted to be. In fact, he was tantalizingly close, less than a mile outside Hale o Lono Harbor, swimming steadily. Just as he was planning his entry, as if specifically to thwart him, the current returned to snatch him away. Again he was whipped toward Lā‘au Point. It was beyond discourag-ing. He was hungry. He anticipated being swept again around the point and to the north of the island. But luck seemed to favor him this time. The current had changed just enough so that he could duck inside the point and hold his position. He'd have to try getting into shore here, but not in the dark through the unpredictable surf. He decided to wait out the night—he would swim against the current and essentially hold his place until the sun rose in a few hours. In the morning, he could look for a way to get to the shore and out of the current boomerang.

Daybreak came. Leo wanted out of the water. He couldn't risk swimming the few miles down to Hale o Lono and getting captured by the current yet again. He was ready to finish this swim once and for all. Half a mile from the point he could see an opening where it looked as if, with luck, he could slip into shore between crashing waves. He swam straight for that opening, and with surprising ease caught two successive waves all the way to shallow water. He dropped his legs and found himself waist deep on rocks. He had made it. It was more than twenty hours since his plane had crashed. He was in the middle of nowhere, but it was less than five miles to the mining outpost at Hale o Lono. He crawled up onto a flat rock, collapsed, and promptly fell asleep.

When he awoke, it was late morning. Slowly and painfully, he picked his way along the coastal rocks and *kiawe* thorns to Hale o Lono. Workers at the harbor looked up in amazement as the bedraggled, bleeding fisherman limped up from the shore. Leo, understated as always, asked for some water. He asked if he could use the phone in their small shack to call for a ride home. The pilot who flew from Honolulu to retrieve him was Bobby Whittinghill. Ohai had risked himself years earlier to rescue the young pilot on that stormy night on Ni'ihau, and now Bobby figured the least he could do was chauffeur his old friend home. By the time they reached

Leo Ohai, O'ahu, 2003

Honolulu, news of Ohai's feat had spread to his pilot friends, some of whom had known better than to give up on the wily fisherman. Several came out to greet him, marveling at his skill and endurance.

Later, at the hospital, Levon Ohai went to visit his father. Leo was banged up and about twenty pounds lighter. His eyes, ravaged by salt water, were red and swollen. But he was otherwise uninjured. He was eager to go home. He hated being cooped up. His son chuckled, and asked him about the accident.

"What happened, Dad?"

The fisherman's mind went back, not to the moment he ditched his plane, but to his conversation with Laole two days earlier.

"I made a promise," he replied, "and then I forgot about what I said."

Leo Ohai recovered and soon returned to his fishing business. He retired from aerial fish-spotting in 1975, turning over that duty to one of his sons, Nephi, but he continues to fish.

Thanksgiving Weekend

Puʻukapukapu, the "forbidden hill," sits sentry over a white-sand beach and sparkling Hawaiian waters that fuse seamlessly with an infinite blue horizon. Set back from Halapē Beach, the Puʻukapukapu cliff towers over a windswept landscape, rising one thousand feet into a rocky knob. From a distance it looks like the raised knuckle on a clenched fish, ready to pound. Its very name connotes a sacred and regal place and a warning to any who might engage in inappropriate behavior there. To underscore what would be ominous enough if stated just once, the name repeats the word *kapu*, meaning both sacred and taboo.

It was at Thanksgiving, in 1975, that a group of hikers discovered the deadly side of the stoic landmark during what was to have been a tranquil holiday camping outing. The campers little suspected as they settled between the mountain and the ocean that Puʻukapukapu was about to unleash its fury in a cascade of boulders, and that its rain of rocks would foreshadow an even greater terror that would rise from the ocean and roar across the land.

Typically there is not much activity around Puʻukapukapu, just the blustery winds that ripple the long grasses on its flanks, blowing them in soft waves that shimmer in rainbow hues of gold, green, and a muted pink. Anchoring one edge of Hawai'i Volcanoes National Park, the hill is a landmark on the scrubby terrain, but it lacks the panache of the dormant craters and the spewing caldera that are the park's star attractions. Like many of Hawai'i's cliff features, Pu'ukapukapu is the remnant of a landslide that saw a huge chunk of land simply tumble to the ocean. It's off the beaten path for tour groups, but backpackers in the know regularly make their way across Pu'ukapukapu and its surrounding volcanic terrain. Over a scenic eight miles, the trail crosses old lava flows where hardy plants and small, twisted trees grow up through the rock, as well as more recent flows with hardened, lumpy black lava that often resembles the loose, wrinkled skin on an elephant's leg. Native flowers dot the ground in bursts of yellow, purple, and melon. Aside from the physical drama of the place, its sheer remoteness lends an aura of ancient times, each boot stride transporting the hiker closer to an age when Hawaiian people lived by fishing and hunting along this southeast coast of the Big Island of Hawai'i.

The National Park Service bills Halapē as a rigorous hike. The reward for those who persevere is a gem of a beach, an oasis dotted with greenery and sandy camping spots alongside incandescent waters. So it was that several groups of hikers made their way to Halapē in 1975, ready for an extended Thanksgiving weekend. Backpacks laden with provisions, they wound over and around Pu'ukapukapu, across the undulating fields of *pili* grasses and down to the welcoming beach.

◇◇◇

Jack Straka was just plain wiped out that evening. He had hiked in with two companions and they were joined by two more, a Dr. Michael Irwin and his son, who, amazingly, trudged into the campsite after dark with a flashlight. How these two made it at night was a mystery to Jack. The terrain was rough enough in the daytime, when at least you could see the rocky trail. Although there were almost no trees on the route, it was sometimes hard to make out the path. Were it not for the stone cairns that Scouts had stacked to mark the trail, it would be easy to lose the way.

Jack, at forty-one, was a newcomer in Hawai'i—what the locals called a *malihini*—arrived from the mainland just a few months earlier. Leaving his job with a New Jersey electronics firm to seek a new life, he had traveled across the country until he found his way to the island state. He took up wood turning and now created fine bowls from Hawaiian woods, the kind that tourists would buy in a gallery or at a craft fair.

Jack had hooked up with the Irwins and his fellow hikers, Elliott and Bob, through the Sierra Club. The Halapē hike was one of many that the club organized for anyone who wanted to sign up, so Jack didn't know his companions well. The group pitched their tents in Halapē's celebrated coconut grove, a refuge at the water's edge where dozens of tall, slender trees rose from the sand. They cooked up some camp food, ate dinner, and settled in for the night.

Jack was immensely relieved they'd be here for a layover day, that he wouldn't have to hike back out tomorrow. He was beat. It wasn't that he was unused to hiking. Jack had been on a number of Sierra Club treks—a good way to socialize and see new places—but this time he wondered if he had bitten off a bit too much. The volcanic terrain and blazing sun had sapped his energy. He felt better after lazing in the water that afternoon, but now he was just plain sore and stiff. Jack took note of a Boy Scout group that was sharing the coconut grove. Some were using a small shelter the Park Service had built, essentially just a tin roof atop rough walls of rock and wood. Its crucial purpose was to serve as a water catchment system for campers, its metal roof slanted to drain rainwater into a large, above-ground cistern. Campers could treat and drink this water, so that they had to carry only one day's water on their backs when hiking in.

On this, his first trip to Halapē, Timothy Twigg-Smith was having the time of his life. He was, at thirteen, one of the younger members of Boy Scout Troop 77 from Hilo. Descended from one of Hawai'i's original missionary families, Timothy had a mop of blond hair and large, dark-rimmed glasses. He had heard a lot about the famous Halapē hike from his fellow Scouts. Troop 77 hiked in every year and did a lot to fix the place up, clearing out palm fronds and building small rock tables. They tried to leave the beach better than they found it. The kids told Timothy that Halapē was a big hike, and hard, but when you got there, it was the greatest. Part of the lore was about a fantastic surf break just offshore next to a tiny islet. The boys thought that it probably had never been ridden. All the kids were avid surfers, but none of them had figured out how to lug a surfboard down this trail when they already were groaning under their backpacks. As it turned out, when the six Scouts and their four adult supervisors arrived hot and dusty on this trip, the scoutmasters gave the boys strict orders to stay near shore, well away from that break and the strong offshore current.

Halapē had another unique feature: Back from the beach a hundred yards or so, but well before Puʻukapukapu began its climb, was a big ditch—called a crack—a thirty-foot-wide split in the earth with high rocky sides, formed by geologic activity. From the air it looked like a giant scar extending to the coast from the shoulder of Puʻukapukapu. Part of the crack was filled with brackish water that made a perfect swimming pool. The Scouts had a great time splashing around in it. After spending all Friday swimming and fishing and racing on the beach, the boys were ready for a sound sleep.

This was a busy weekend at Halapē. Several other hikers and some fishermen on horseback arrived, thirty-four campers in all including the Scouts and Jack's group. The adults with Troop 77 had dropped their packs when they reached the coconut grove. One boy, David White, stayed there with his father, Don, and the other men. The Scout leaders permitted Michael Stearns, the senior patrol leader, to take Timothy and three other boys across a patch of rocky coast that curved closer to Puʻukapukapu—about a ten-minute walk from the coconut grove. This was Boulder Bay, a place littered with the rocky castoffs from the shudders of Puʻukapukapu in years past. Here there was another open-sided shed, not far from the water. The boys set up camp there, careful to hang their backpacks and shoes from the rafters. Nobody wanted to wake up with a centipede in his boot or rats rummaging through the snacks in his backpack.

It was just before 4 A.M. when the campers were rattled awake. The ground was shaking, with the rolling, rumbling sensation that the island locals knew well. The boys peered from their sleeping bags into the darkness. On the Big Island, the most geologically active of the Hawaiian chain, they were used to these temblors, which mostly were linked to the island's volcanic activity, rather than the movement of tectonic plates that caused earthquakes elsewhere. In fact, thousands of quakes rattled the Big Island every year, only a few of them strong enough to be noticed by the general population. Over the last century, the greatest concentration of Big Island quakes had occurred on the southern flank of the Kīlauea volcano—along the coast that included Halapē. Back in 1868, a major quake had wiped out a village near here and unleashed a tsunami that hammered the coast with waves up to forty-five feet high.

Timothy grabbed for his glasses, which he had placed next to his sleeping bag. Immediately aware that this was a quake, he looked toward Kīlauea in the distance to see if there might be any danger from a lava flow. No red lava was visible. The boys milled around, talking excitedly. The quake had rocked them pretty well, more so than a milder one the night before. But they decided it wasn't that big a deal, not serious enough to consult with their Scout leaders in the coconut grove. Over there the campers were awakened also, but eventually everyone returned to the sleeping bags and drifted back to sleep.

Their dreams ended a little more than an hour later, abruptly obliterated by a wide-awake nightmare. The ground rumbled violently, like a runaway train roaring beneath the earth. They tried to stand, but the force of the quake threw them to the ground. They crawled and wobbled out of their tents. It was 4:48 A.M. Seismologists would measure this temblor at 7.2 on the Richter scale—a major earthquake and the most powerful one to hit Hawai'i since 1868.

Unlike the Scouts, Jack had never felt an earthquake. Unnerved and powerless against the shaking, he sat on the ground. He heard boulders, hurled by Puʻukapukapu, slamming to the ground behind the coconut grove. They crashed with terrifying, loud bangs. Jack looked through the darkness and saw that none were close enough to reach his campsite. He turned to the ocean. Down the coast, to the south, he saw blue flashes on the horizon. Must be power lines broken apart by the quake, he thought nervously.

Over at Boulder Bay, Timothy was rocked side to side. He tried to stand up and dropped his glasses. He couldn't afford to lose them. He groped for them unsteadily, then clenched them in his fist. His legs instinctively wanted to run, but he was instantly knocked to the ground. He was on his hands and knees in front of the shelter, anchored by a powerful force. Everyone was yelling. The sound from Puʻukapukapu was deafening. The boulders crashed close behind the campsite, rock against rock, like the sound of a thousand construction trucks dumping their loads all at once. Mike was trying to herd everyone behind the shelter to protect them from the bouncing rocks. The shaking went on and on before it finally let up enough for the boys to stand and catch their breaths, their attention focused on the boulders that were still dropping from the cliff. In the lull, they raced to untie their boots hanging inside the shed, in hopes of sprinting to the adults in the coconut grove. Timothy allowed himself to think tentatively that everything was fine. Then he heard water. He glanced to the sea. Gosh, the surf came up, he thought. Before he could grasp what was happening, someone was yelling.

"The water! The water!"

Timothy looked up again and focused this time. He saw white water surging. It was unreal. He had never seen a wave that huge. It was almost on him, looming above his head, not like a clean-breaking surfing wave, but a wall of rushing water, whooshing inland—very fast. He had a split second to whip off his glasses and grasp them securely in his hand. He took a breath. The water swooped him, like a primal surfing wipeout but bigger and faster than anything he had ever felt. He knew the wave would take him at will. His experience with the ocean told him he was completely helpless against this power. He was terrified.

Tsunamis were not a frequent occurrence, but Hawai'i did have a long history of them. By 1975, the state had a tsunami warning system that monitored faraway ocean disturbances—earthquakes or landslides—that could trigger tsunamis. The equipment tracked waves that might end up coming ashore as tsunamis in Hawai'i. It was designed to target the wave action in plenty of time to sound alarms and start coastal evacuations. Elaborate evacuation plans were part of Hawai'i's civil defense, geared to get people out of the inundation zones. There was one hitch: the system didn't have time to warn about locally generated tsunamis. If a nearby earthquake, rather than one in Alaska or Japan, for instance, triggered a tsunami, it would be onshore before the monitoring systems knew it was coming. This was what befell the Big Island in 1975. The epicenter of the earthquake was offshore, just fifteen miles west of Halapē—very close from a seismic perspective.

The ocean blasted Timothy into the shelter and shoved him out the back wall, collapsing the structure as it flowed. Sharp rocks and thickly branched bushes clawed at him as he was dragged across the ground. He smashed into a large bush. Now he felt the force of the water rushing past and over him as the branches held him. He was holding his breath, stuck in the bush, unable to move beneath the water. Just as it seemed the force was letting up, a second surge raged over him. Timothy was pinned. Still he held his breath, panicky but determined to live through this thing. He fought, but he was out of air. He was drowning. The hand that was clenched around his glasses now loosened, allowing the water to snatch them away. Timothy gave in to the power. Complete relaxation came over him, a calm like nothing he had known. Strangely, his eyes began to see a bright white light. He watched it, peaceful and unworried.

I'm just stuck here in the bush, he thought.

It was no big deal, almost a relief, in fact. He was now floating lightly in the water. And then—the water receded. Ripping into his timeless moment, it dragged at him, trying to yank him seaward with it. But the bush would not surrender him. Air filled his lungs.

◇◇◇

In the coconut grove, Jack saw the wall of water right after the shaking subsided. He heard his own voice.

"Tidal wave!"

Near him, the Irwins and Bob were running.

Jack couldn't run. He had been stricken with polio as a child, and the muscles of his left leg and right arm had been weakened. He could hike, but he couldn't run. Jack threw his arms around a coconut tree, determined to shinny up and hang on above the watery onslaught. Before he could haul himself up, however, he felt two arms locked around both him and the tree. It was Elliott. Jack opened his mouth to tell his friend to let him go up the tree. Before he uttered a word, the sea engulfed them, climbing from their ankles so quickly that the force ripped them from the tree even as the water climbed to their heads. Now Jack was pushed under, tumbled and banged across the rocky ground. He got a gulp of air and went under again. Time seemed to pass slowly.

This is it, he thought.

He was going to die here. There was something matter of fact about it. He swallowed water, unable to breathe. Just as suddenly, he found himself popping to the surface. He gulped air. He was floating in darkness. Where the hell was he? He looked around and realized that he was down in the crack where the kids had been swimming earlier. The wave that had dumped him here was receding. The crack had saved Jack from being swept out with it. There was no sign of Elliott or Bob. Dr. Irwin's son was at the edge of the crack. Jack also was aware of a Boy Scout scurrying past.

"Here comes another wave," someone shouted.

Jack needed to get out of this pit before he got pummeled again. He would head toward Pu'ukapukapu, away from the ocean, he thought. He tried to climb up the side, but the wall was gravelly and steep. He fell back. To his relief the incoming wave fell short of the crack this time. He focused his mind on mustering the strength to get out of this ditch. He made his way to a *kiawe* tree that had washed in, and used its branches to haul himself up and over the side. After making sure no more waves were inbound, he collapsed by the edge of the crack. His friends were near, except for Elliott. They called for Elliott and he hollered back. He was okay and was helping one of the Scout leaders who was hurt. The campers, Jack realized, were scattered all along the crack. Jack was in bad shape himself. Exhausted before the tsunami came ashore, he was now completely spent. He checked himself over for damage. Nothing seemed broken. His fingers found a hole in one ankle, but he had no pain there because this ankle had undergone a surgery years earlier, rendering it without feeling. He felt mostly just beat up and tired. There was no sign of the camping gear. Everything had been washed away. As the shorefront breezes brought a chill to the wet campers, Jack and his friends sat back to back to stay warm and wait out the night.

From his perch in the bush, Timothy heard someone yelling. The other boys were nearby. Even with his blurry vision, he could see in the darkness that blood was dripping down Mike's face. Timothy managed to tumble free of the bush, dazed. All the boys were stunned, trying to collect themselves. They wanted only to get out of there before any more waves hit. Two boys went to check on their friends at the coconut grove while Timothy and the other two scrambled barefoot across the rough landscape. Scratched by bushes and rocks, they stumbled through the dark in search of high ground. They were joined by three fishermen. After almost a mile, near where the trail began climbing more steeply, the fishermen continued hiking out while the boys decided they had traveled far enough to wait out the darkness.

Dawn brought a grim inventory. The hikers took stock. Two campers were dead, among them a Hilo surgeon named James Mitchel, who was one of the Scout leaders. The other was one of the fishermen, who was nowhere to be found and was presumed claimed by the sea. Nearly all the other campers on the Halapē side had been saved in the crack. Initially they were pinned there by the force of the wave pouring on top of them, but when it receded, they were left in the crevice nursing an array of injuries and bruises. The shelters were gone, along with the water tank and tents, anything loose in the water's path. Penetrating some three hundred feet inland, the waves had dumped a cache of debris in the crack. The offshore islet was underwater. Halapē Beach itself had sunk more than ten feet, and the grand coconut grove was awash. The trees were half buried in surf that over time would claim the entire grove, leaving only a few white stumps poking up from the newly reconfigured shoreline.

David White, despite his own injuries, was ministering to his father, who was badly hurt, with a partially collapsed lung and severe abrasions. White said he was dying and urged his son to leave him for safer ground. But the boy refused, remaining to keep his father warm until help arrived. He used his own body warmth, and covered his father with *pili* grass, the hardy weed used by early missionaries in mattresses and for crude thatch construction. One Scout, Leif Thompson, was assisting James Kawakami, another adult with the Scout group, who had suffered internal injuries. Leif gave him water to drink and built a windbreak from wood and rocks to protect the man from the brisk breeze.

Eventually, Jack saw a helicopter in the distance. To his dismay, it did not come close to the group huddled at Halapē. Then they heard the unmistakable buzz of a small plane and looked up to see it flying above them. It was a Hilo pilot surveying the damage. They waved frantically. He circled and dipped his wings. He had seen them. Soon an Army helicopter choppered into view, alerted by the Hilo pilot that there were people to be rescued at Halapē. As it touched down, the chopper's thwacking blades shattered the quiet that had settled over the stricken landscape. To the campers' ears, it was a welcome ruckus. Jack, barefoot and rendered barely able to

Jack Straka, Big Island, 2003

Timothy Twigg-Smith (second from right) with Boy Scout Troop 77, Big Island,
November 29, 1975. Photo courtesy of The Pacific Tsunami Museum.

move by the night's ordeal, could not make it to the chopper on his own. A crew member grabbed him around the waist to support him. He winced in pain as the man's rough gloves touched the ripped flesh on his bare side. But Jack wasn't complaining. Now he could stop worrying about where he would find the energy to get himself out of there. He would make it. He settled stiffly into the helicopter, aware of little more than his own overwhelming relief. Rising above the landscape, the helicopter abandoned the rock-strewn coast and waterlogged coconut trees. It ferried the hikers, a handful at a time, to safety. As the sun rose in the sky, Puʻukapukapu stood silent sentry.

Timothy Twigg-Smith recovered quickly from his scrapes and was soon back in the water, surfing, fishing, and diving. He revisited Halapē years later, and now lives on Oʻahu. Jack Straka spent a few days in the hospital, and soon went back to hiking and four-wheel exploration. Along the shore, he always makes sure to keep an eye seaward. He still lives on the Big Island. Leif Thompson and David White were decorated by the Boy Scouts with the National Medal of Merit.

Ticket to Nowhere

The night sky was clear and vast, melding with the ocean in a giant spray of stars and whitecaps like a dusting of silver across the universe. The panorama enveloped Jon Stockton, a speck of a dot in the middle of the sea. The water, finally approaching calm, twinkled all around him. Jon thought his salt-smeared eyes were deceiving him. The sea looked weirdly electrified, lit by streaks and flashes as his paddle strokes agitated thousands of minute organisms, creating bioluminescence. Overhead, the Milky Way sprawled across the sky in a lavender hue, the brightness illuminating shadowy clouds that kept morphing into animal-like shapes. Lulled by the rocking of the ocean, Jon felt spaced out. He was floating in the great galaxy. He was one with all of it. For the wave-battered kayaker, his body and mind ravaged by fatigue and exposure, the night was almost soothing. He tried to be positive.

I guess it's not a bad way to go, he thought.

After all the pain and bottomless exhaustion he had endured on this kayaking trip, he ultimately was doing what he loved. Now he drifted in and out of catnaps punctuated by splashes of salt water in his eyes. He awoke to daylight, grayish skies and a brisk wind that nearly flipped his kayak—again. Jon wept for thirty minutes straight.

◇◇◇

Jonathan Stockton had arrived on the west shore of the Big Island of Hawai'i a week earlier, excited about his solo kayak trip up the west coast of the island state's biggest land mass. The journey was bittersweet because it marked a directional change in his life. Until a few months earlier he had been living in Hawai'i, developing a training program for would-be missionaries based on what he had learned in his world travels and teaching experiences. He had first visited Hawai'i as a college student in a mission program, and subsequently traveled in Australia, Asia, and Latin America. He taught English and began a life of Christian mission work. But during a visit to his home state of Arizona the previous Christmas, he was offered, and accepted, a position at a church that his late father had helped to found. After a great deal of thought, he now was moving back to Phoenix.

In July 2002, he returned to Hawai'i to tie up loose ends. The trip had a side benefit—it would feed his thirst for adventure. Tall and athletic, Jon at twenty-eight was an avid outdoorsman, a former high school wrestler who was always up for a challenge whether it was whitewater kayaking in Oregon or prowling the backcountry of Hawai'i. During his earlier time on the Big Island, he had hiked and dived and reveled in waterfall-leaping expeditions with a friend's sons. Once while surfing he had endured a potentially deadly attack by a phalanx of clinging, stinging jellyfish that left him nearly unable to move. Now, on this trip, he was trying out a new Klepper folding kayak outfitted with a mast and spinnaker sail. Seventeen feet long and three feet wide, it was easy to handle, constructed with a light wood frame and a high-tech fabric. Deemed nearly indestructible, it could nonetheless be disassembled and packed into a shoulder bag.

Jon would start just south of the Keāhole-Kona airport and run up along the baked-lava coast past some of Hawaiʻi's most lavish resort hotels. He would paddle north along the Kawaihae coast, an area steeped in cultural and historic significance from the days of King Kamehameha, the voyaging Captain Cook, and the once thriving sugar industry. He then would round the hornlike tip of the Big Island and drop down along the northeast side to paddle his last several miles into the remote Kohala region, where he had left belongings with a friend. The journey was about eighty miles in all, and Jon planned between seven and ten days to complete it. He packed camping gear and provisions that wouldn't weigh him down: beef jerky, trail mix, dried foods. He'd keep two gallons of water in the kayak, and his cellular phone in a waterproof bag.

On Wednesday morning he launched under sunny skies. With a slight wind at his back, he clocked a respectable ten miles to his campsite. The next day he surprised himself by pushing even farther, all the way to the posh Mauna Kea Beach Hotel, a day ahead of schedule. He checked into the hotel for the night. Friday morning dawned benign enough, but word at the hotel was that a storm was building on the north side of the island. Jon watched the weather report on TV. Unfazed, he downed a big breakfast and then fetched his kayak. Localized storms were not that unusual in this area, and were often generated by winds whipping around the Mauna Kea summit. He'd be close enough to shore, not more than one hundred yards out, to hurry in if need be.

The day's itinerary had him traveling another twenty miles, the most ambitious day of the trip. Jon made good time, but kept an eye to the northern point where the storm clouds gathered. About four in the afternoon, the wind picked up as he rounded a bend about half a mile from his destination, Māhukona Beach, where he had gone fishing and diving many times. What he saw alarmed him. A fierce wind was bearing down in visible sheets on the water. He quickly trimmed and fastened his sails, turning to make a beeline for the shore.

Conditions rapidly turned ugly. Billowing from the darkened sky, the storm bore down on him as he paddled southward. He leaned into his rudder to turn the boat to shore, but he could feel the storm pushing him out. He thought about his choices. He could either try and flee ahead of the storm to sunny Kona, near where he started his trip, or fight the wind and waves to paddle in to shore. Jon had no chance to deliberate. A full-force gust slapped his kayak and flipped it. He was in the water. He clutched at the kayak, thankful for the life vest he wore over his longsleeved shirt. But the storm, manageable just minutes earlier, worsened by the second. Desperation crept over him. Perhaps he should leave the boat and try to swim for shore. He figured it would take about six hours to cross the rough sea. Or he could stay with the upside-down kayak and try to ride out the storm. Maybe he'd be able to hoist the sail and paddle to safety in the morning. That seemed the safer option. He managed to right the boat, but it was still filled with water, pitching and rolling in the wild waves. The sea's furious effort to claim the boat was thwarted only by the air sponsons that ran lengthwise along its sides. Jon hung on to the side and looked back to the fast-receding island. As he flowed out to the fierce channel that separated Maui and the Big Island, fear coursed through him, a panic he had never known. In a few brief minutes, he had turned from a confident adventurer into a helpless boater, dragged into the channel and the night. He began to pray. He asked for guidance, direction, calm. Over the island, a rainbow appeared, arcing from the darkness to the sunny side.

It was a signal, a sign of hope, Jon thought. He could live through this.

Then, with the sun dropping low in the sky, he saw a large container ship push off from Kawaihae Harbor. It was heading straight for him, five hundred, four hundred, three hundred yards. Jon clambered onto his upside-down kayak and waved at the ship, but couldn't keep his balance. The ship let out a long blast like a foghorn. Jon's heart leapt. The ship saw him and was signaling him! The vessel, however, turned toward Maui and disappeared on the northern horizon. The sun sank along with Jon's spirits.

The storm swirled as darkness clamped down on the ocean. One following another, the waves rose to twenty feet above Jon's head, monsters looming from the darkness to pound the waterlogged kayak and its captain. The kayak was tossed like a bath toy in the wind-whipped water. Jon fought his panic.

Keep it together! he yelled to himself.

He hollered at the waters to be still in the name of Jesus. A wave nailed him in the face. He had to get hold of himself. He didn't know how he would make it, but this would be the longest night of his life. Just holding on was a challenge. After an hour gripping the boat, his hand was so numb that he couldn't make a fist. He wedged his arm painfully between the seat and the side to keep from slipping away. Still, the force of the waves knocked him free. Each time he struggled back, grabbing the spare oar and other items that were breaking loose from the kayak. He tried wrapping himself around the kayak, his back to the oncoming swells, so the waves would push him toward the boat instead of ripping him away.

The conditions invited hypothermia, the water and wind combining to chill his body, a danger he now recognized as imminent. He concentrated on getting into the boat and emptying it, hoping to dry off enough to fend off hypothermia, and maybe even steer the boat. If he could just use his bilge pump to empty the water, he could try to surf the waves. But each time he tried, another wave defeated him.

The hours dragged by. His wedged arm was killing him. His efforts began to seem so futile, like those of a man hanging from a cliff, just waiting for his muscles to give out. But he began studying the way the cresting waves would tip the boat up and dump out most of the water before refilling it. He devised a plan to use that rolling motion to scoop himself into the kayak in the second before it filled up again. After an hour of exhausting, unsuccessful attempts, he landed himself in the boat. He pumped water furiously until the kayak responded to the rudder and his body movement. Now he could ride the waves.

It was crazy, he thought. Here he was surfing two-story monsters that normally he'd never go near. The night was endless.

At sunup, the sky was still overcast and the sea rough. In the ten miles that separated Jon from the shore was a minefield of violent swells. The tourist center of Kona was about forty miles to the south, bathed in sunshine. Jon decided he'd be better off making the run south, especially since the north coast was thinly populated. Up on this part of the island, he never could get a cell phone signal, even on land. Newly resolved, he picked up an oar and paddled south.

Three aching hours later, a wave flipped him. Struggling to right the kayak, he saw his worst nightmare. The middle pole of his three-part mast was gone, vanished into the churning waters. He still had the other two sections, but without the middle, the sail was useless. Until now, he had harbored the idea that his misfortune could turn out like a great adventure, culminating with the Klepper's triumphant return to shore under sail once the storm abated. Any chance of that Hollywood storyline was now vanquished. The wind and the currents were conspiring to defeat him. Trying to get out of this channel would be the most grueling paddle he'd ever known, he thought. All he had was his waning strength, and his will.

He dug in, pushing beyond fatigue until his arms were like noodles. Every time the kayak capsized, it was a twenty-five-minute struggle to right it again. He tried to fuel himself with some beef jerky and dried pineapple, but they were so contaminated with salt water that he vomited. He would have to ration his water and eat as little as possible. He knew his body could not afford to lose the liquid.

As the day wore on, sleepiness overcame him. His arms felt ready to fall off, but he couldn't afford to lose ground to the current. Afraid of nodding off, he set his watch alarm to go off every few minutes. The swells diminished as the day waned, and as dusk bled into darkness Jon pushed his paddle through the water on grit alone, little by little conquering the distance to shore. At 2 A.M. he was close enough to see the lights of the marina at Kona. Relief bubbled within him. If he could get close enough, he might be able to get a cellular signal. He would make it to Kona—if only he could keep from collapsing under the crushing weight of fatigue. He decided to set his alarm so he could nap for two or three minutes, and then paddle for five minutes. Each time he forced his eyes awake he found he had moved a little farther south of his angle into the marina.

Get a grip, he told himself. *Stop slacking off. You'll die out here if you don't shape up.*

At 4 A.M. a strong offshore wind picked up. Jon battled it with everything he had left.

He awoke, his face taut with sunburn and saltwater exposure. He was lying flat across his kayak. He looked to the island. The marina was faded from sight. Through a haze, he saw Mauna Kea, at 13,796 feet the highest summit in Hawai'i. Nothing else. Jon's heart dropped to the depths of the sea. He was at least thirty miles offshore, rolling in big waves. It was Sunday morning and the storm had abated, but he had missed his chance. Furious at himself, he picked up his paddle, pointed himself at the island, directly into the wind, and lifted his arms. Stroke after stroke, his battered arms dragged the paddle through the water. Breaking out of the channel was agonizing. By midday, he was spent. The water was calm enough for him to pause and, for the first time since the storm, clamber to the front of the kayak where he had stashed his gear—and his phone. In desperation, he pulled out the phone and switched it on, not really expecting results. When the power flashed on, he couldn't believe his eyes. The display indicated a signal. Quickly he dialed 9-1-1. He heard the faint voice of the emergency operator. His heart pounded.

"My name is Jon Stockton. I'm hypothermic. I'm thirty miles off the coast. I need rescue right away," he blurted.

She couldn't hear him. Call back, she said. He dialed again.

"I'm out to sea. Capsized off Māhukona. Get the Coast Guard! Coast Guard! Coast Guard!" he yelled.

◈◈◈

Petty Officer Justin Acosta was busy with a boat that had reported engine trouble near Pearl Harbor when the phone on his desk rang at 12:43 P.M. He had arrived at the Coast Guard command center early that Sunday morning ready for his usual twenty-four-hour shift. Justin was the search-and-rescue coordinator in the windowless center, which was located on Sand Island just off the busy Nimitz Highway in Honolulu. While a colleague talked to boats coming in and out of Hawai'i's various harbors, picking up distress calls and mayday calls, Justin planned and coordinated all the rescues, dispatching the Coast Guard's fleet of boats, helicopters, and planes. At twenty-three Justin was newly married, a Hawai'i native who had joined the Coast Guard five years earlier. He was attracted to the service partly because he'd be stationed near water, where he could pursue his passion for surfing. He was trained as a navigator on Coast Guard cutters, and he was proud of his local knowledge of the Hawaiian Islands, things like pidgin language and local place names. It came in handy in dealing with boaters in these waters. Justin was serious about his work, initially treating every call, no matter how far-fetched, as if it were a real emergency. Lives depended on his efficiency.

He reached for the phone. This number was in the phone book as the Coast Guard's twenty-four-hour line. You never could tell who might be on the other end. Sometimes people wanted directions to the *Arizona* Memorial at Pearl Harbor. Sometimes it was a boater in trouble. On this Sunday, it was the fire department over on the Big Island. They had a distress call from a guy named Jon Stockton whose red kayak had capsized off Māhukona. He had given the dispatcher some rough coordinates as to where he thought he was, and the fire department retrieved his phone number. Justin looked at the coordinates.

This didn't make sense.

The coordinates were nowhere near Māhukona. In fact, they put Jon far south on the opposite side of the island. Perhaps with the wind interference and the weak cellular connection, the emergency operator had not heard the numbers correctly. Justin replotted the position, assuming a slight numerical variation that at least would put the coordinates on the west side of the island—but the new position was far south and way out in the ocean. Justin dialed Jon's cell phone number. Instead of the kayaker, he reached a recorded answer. He left his number and said the Coast Guard stood ready to help as needed. Then he called Barbers Point near Honolulu, where the Coast Guard aircraft were based. He didn't want to lose time waiting for Jon to pick up his message, minutes or hours in which the kayak would only drift farther out, and his aircraft would need an hour to get to the Big Island.

He launched a helicopter and a C-130 search plane. The plane flew south to the middle of nowhere, where Justin had speculated Jon's coordinates were. The helicopter flew north, offshore from Māhukona. Both aircraft flew in the tight grid patterns that were standard for these searches. Spotting something as small as a kayak on the open ocean could be breathtakingly difficult, but Justin felt confident. Coast Guard fliers trained for this.

Hours later, both aircraft reported back to him that they had nothing. They had so little information about where they should be looking. Justin could offer them no new instructions unless Jon called him back. At 5:30 P.M. the phone rang.

After talking to the fire department, Jon had paddled vigorously in search of a better connection. He heard his phone beep in the front of the boat. He grabbed it and retrieved Justin's message. The Coast Guard! Praying for another connection, he dialed, jabbing his aching fingers at the keypad. Justin answered. There was a lot of wind, but he could hear the kayaker's voice.

"I'm Jon Stockton. I got in trouble off Māhukona. I'm farther south . . . "

The phone disconnected. This couldn't be happening, Jon thought. He could not be this close to rescue and lose his only chance. Frantic, he dialed again. Nothing. He tried repeatedly without success. He paddled furiously for the island. Closer to land had to mean a stronger signal. He dialed again, and again.

Elated to make contact with Jon at last, Justin could do nothing but wait after the phone went dead. He tried calling back but got the message service, establishing the pattern of the next few hours. Jon could make calls out, but incoming calls reached only his answering machine. Fifteen minutes went by. The phone rang again. This time Jon poured out his story quickly. He was well south of Kona now. He'd been out there for three days, caught in a storm. He had little food or water. The phone went dead again. Now began a series of brief calls over high wind, each one disconnected after less than a minute. Justin asked if Jon if he had seen aircraft. Jon had seen nothing. That confirmed he was well south of Kona, Justin thought. Otherwise he should have seen flights from the airport, all of which would be going north from Kona. Now Justin knew he needed to redirect the aircraft, but where was Jon?

"What can you see on the island?" he asked.

Jon could see the tops of both Mauna Kea and Mauna Loa, the two highest mountains on Hawai'i Island. He saw those summits above the clouds, and the observatory atop Mauna Kea. Not much else. Justin was amazed. That description put Jon maybe as far as forty miles out. If he were closer, he'd see the mountains below the clouds. Justin was perplexed. How were the calls getting through? Even on a boat less than twenty miles out, Justin could never get a cellular phone signal. Maybe Jon was closer than he thought he was. What Justin knew for certain was that this guy was in real trouble. He could tell by Jon's voice that there was no hoax here. The question was, where was he? Could he have drifted across the channel to Maui, an unlikely scenario but one that would put him in view of Haleakalā summit?

No, Jon told Justin.

He knew what Haleakalā looked like. It had steeper sides than the long, gradual slopes of the Big Island volcanoes. Justin thought about the current running southwest, and winds blowing north. Computer analysis factoring in the countereffect of the wind showed he should be moving northwest, but Justin's gut and the fact that Jon saw no flights from the airport told him the kayak was southwest of Kona. Justin just hoped Jon wasn't drifting beyond the southern shore of the island. The Big Island was the southernmost in the Hawaiian archipelago, jumping-off point to Tahiti, some 2,750 miles away. If they didn't find him, Jon would be carried into the vast Pacific Ocean, with nothing but a few dots of islands between him and French Polynesia, or New Zealand if he drifted farther west.

The sun was about to go down. Justin was running out of questions for Jon, but somehow he had to get more concrete information for the pilots. He thought about all of his experience scouting surf spots around the islands, his observations on how the sun rose and set. He told Jon to face the setting sun and describe the location of the mountaintops in relation to his body. Jon said the mountains were at his right shoulder. That was what Justin needed to know. If he were west or north of Kona, the mountains would be at his back.

Save your battery, Justin told him, and call when you see a plane.

He sent his aircraft south.

Jon waited, scouring the skies in the fading light. He was parched, hoarding the bit of water he had left. He felt better just knowing that at least someone was out there looking for him. If only he could help them find him. Finally, he saw it—a plane off in the distance. It looked to be halfway between his kayak and the island. Excitedly, he grabbed his phone and dialed Justin's number. The display read "test mode." This couldn't be.

Please, please let me get through, he prayed.

The plane flew away from him and disappeared. He heard the dial tone, and then ringing.

"Jon?" came Justin's voice.

"I saw a plane go by two minutes ago!" Jon yelled.

Justin told him to again face the setting sun and describe the plane's location in relation to himself and the mountains. His reply again told Justin to send his planes farther south and west. Several minutes passed. Jon called again. He had seen a plane but again it took him a couple of minutes to get the phone connection. Justin told him to hang in there.

"We're going to find you. Stay positive."

Justin didn't know what else to say. Here he was sitting in a comfortable office, out of the elements, and this kayaker who had dropped into his life just hours ago was out there hurting and weak, facing another night of uncertainty and counting on him. Justin just wanted to give the guy hope.

"Call back when you see the plane," he told him.

It would be their last conversation. Jon did see the plane again, and again. He waved and screamed. His phone battery was dead.

The Coast Guard plane, equipped with infrared equipment and night-vision goggles, continued the search in darkness, but it had to return to Oʻahu to change crews. It was 2 A.M. by the time the plane resumed searching. Justin anticipated good news at any moment. They were so close, and his experience told him they had to find this guy. But the hours passed with no word. It was time to look for some help beyond his professional training and knowledge. Justin stepped away from his station and closed the bathroom door. He prayed to God.

Jon waited. He strapped two emergency lights onto his head. He was wiped out, his arms rubbed raw from the friction of his shirt when he paddled. He was so desperate for sleep that he wanted to risk capsizing just for a five-minute nap. But the waves wouldn't give him a break. They tossed stinging salt water into his face every time his eyes closed. He sprawled over the kayak with his arms and legs dangling, trying to keep the boat balanced while resting his body. Deep in the night, he felt a heavy thud. Something whacked the kayak hard. Jon didn't have to wonder—he knew what it was. Sharks were rampant in these waters. Petrified, he pulled in his feet—bleeding from coral cuts—and sat up in the raft. He paddled urgently, now hyper-aware of the danger he faced every time he capsized. He was just a juicy piece of meat out here. A plane flew over. He kept paddling, fading in and out of semisleep.

At sunrise, the helicopter went back out. The whole Coast Guard command was in early, everyone buzzing about the search. Justin, still believing they would spot Jon any time now, decided to stick around after his shift was up at 7:30. Briefing everyone, he deflected any suggestion that this could be a hoax. He knew what he had heard in Jon's voice.

The planes that Jon had seen were around forty miles offshore. Someone suggested asking the phone company if it was possible to pinpoint the cellular calls. Oddly, the record showed Jon's last calls had been made on Friday. The company later said that there had been a glitch between his Arizona service and the records in Hawai'i, and that the cellular towers, although not designed for offshore coverage, conceivably could reach Jon at thirty or more miles depending on circumstances. Based on his own experience, however, Justin couldn't imagine such a thing.

The search area was expanding over hundreds of square miles, and now the navy was called in to help, using its planes, which had the advantage of flying long hours without refueling. With computer data still showing Jon in a northwest drift, the search area was extended north as well as south. Around 11 A.M., Justin went home to sleep, confident that when he awoke later in the day, he would hear good news.

Daylight on Monday morning had arrived with the drone of airplane engines over the ocean. Jon spotted the first of several overflights. He just needed to drift in a predictable path, he thought, and hope they could spot him somehow. One plane made a turn and seemed to head back to him, but flew off again. He could feel himself weakening, bone tired and dehydrated, as the hours rolled by and he drifted into fantasy. He was on a yacht, recounting his adventure to a rapt girl in a bikini. He was sipping a thirst-quenching mai tai. A salty splash in the face snapped him to reality. But now there was a Japanese guy with him on the kayak, probably someone from that container ship out of Kawaihae. Jon yelled at him to get an oar, to take his turn paddling.

"Give me the oar," the guy said.

Jon started. The boat was empty. He was losing it.

Get it together, he told himself.

But he felt unable to function. His neck was as weak as liquid. He knew his chances were fading with the day and the island that was gradually disappearing from view. He roused himself to try and figure a way to get his sail working. But the more he tried to untangle the ropes and rig it the more uncontrollable it was. He gave up. He needed to conserve his strength. As his fourth day at sea slipped away, he saw a plane and couldn't even rouse himself to wave. Sure enough, it flew right over him. That night was clear and calm. He was able to drowse here and there. In his wakeful moments he lay back and felt himself part of the cosmos. He thought he was imagining the bioluminescence in the water. All around him were strange groaning sounds, like low, anguished, even otherwordly cries.

What is this? Jon thought.

It all seemed to preview his doom, and he didn't see how he could make it. In the morning when the wind picked up again, he surrendered to his emotions and cried uncontrollably. Gone was any shred of confidence or bravado. His organs seemed to be shutting down. He was out of water. Mauna Kea had disappeared. This was it. Alone in the endless ocean, he struggled for hollow-sounding breaths. He had never felt so humbled.

How could he hang on for another day, another hour?

In his gear was a book about someone who took a Klepper across the Atlantic, and he was planning to use the pages to write the will that he now had drawn up in his mind, leaving things to his mother, his brothers. He opened the book to write, but closed it. He would do that in his last coherent moments. He pulled himself up in the kayak seat. Chafed and sunburned, he felt like one big bruise. He turned again to prayer, and what came back to him was a strong message that he would live and not die.

How could that be? He was already dying.

But this was the time to dig down and live his beliefs. He pulled out a small plastic-covered Bible, water soaked but legible.

"I lift my eyes to the hills. From where does my help come? My help comes from the Lord," he read from the Psalms. And, "The Lord will keep you from all evil. He will keep your life."

He read on. The Pslams gave him solace, and the words seemed to focus his mind.

What if the Coast Guard called off the search? he thought. His death would be a terrible blow to his mother and two brothers, who were still grieving over his father's death four years earlier. He prayed again, emptied of everything but his prayer to live. He told God he would give up anything, would become a monk, would surrender material things, whatever he could trade for his life. Jon looked over his right shoulder. A plane was sweeping up over the horizon.

◇◇◇

Gary Phillips had learned about the missing kayaker on the Sunday evening news and assumed he'd be in on the search this week. Gary was a radio operator on board a P-3C Orion, a navy maritime patrol aircraft out of Kāneʻohe Bay on the other side of Oʻahu from where Justin worked in the Coast Guard command center. The P-3 was designed for antisubmarine warfare, but its long-range fuel capability made it valuable for search and rescue, and the navy often assisted in Coast Guard searches. On Monday night, Phillips got the call: he'd be flying with the searchers the next day.

The P-3 set off at first light Tuesday. Gary, an aviation warfare systems operator, assumed the kayak was too small to show up on radar, so he took up one of seven stations looking out the window. The plane dropped to about five hundred feet. The crew of twelve rotated in shifts from window to window, one group sleeping while seven others looked into the vast blueness. Whoever spotted the speck of red would yell for the pilot to mark the position so the plane could find it again.

Gazing down, Gary thought the conditions weren't too bad.

Mercifully, there were few whitecaps, making it easier to spot the red kayak and the yellow rain jacket if that moment arrived. Gary tried to envision it, imagining how it would appear from five hundred feet. He watched hours of water, like a movie reel flashing by his window. He was used to seeing nothing for hours on end and he knew it wasn't as futile as it might seem. With the naked eye, you could see things as small as a dolphin from this altitude. The splashing of water would draw the eye.

But the intense watch was physically and mentally draining. The searchers were trained to fight off the sleep their bodies ultimately would crave, and Gary reminded the others that anyone who did reach that point should turn over his window to a replacement. Even the droop of an eye could cost Jon his life. Gary worried about what they might find. It certainly was possible that they would eventually spot the kayak but that Jon would have succumbed to the ravages of four days of exposure. Gary was praying that it wouldn't happen that way.

Then, in a split second, everything changed. Just as he had envisioned, there was the flash of red, the yellow dot in the middle.

"Mark our position! Mark our position! I see him!" Gary hollered.

Jon's hopes escalated when the plane flew closer to him. But it disappeared again. He tried to gauge where it might show up. He paddled in that direction. It reappeared and zoomed over him.

Let it come back, he prayed.

He noticed a dark storm that was building offshore. He couldn't face that again. A half hour went by, each second stitched to the next by Jon's growing desperation and anxiety. Then he saw the plane coming straight for him, its fumes sweeping hazy wrinkles in the air.

He pulled out his silvery, plastic ground cover, a moisture barrier for camping, and fastened it to an oar like a big flapping flag. He took off his yellow rain jacket and waved it around. This plane was approaching him more directly than any had so far. He pressed every fiber of his ravaged body into his mental prayer:

Let them see me, let them see me.

He heard the engines shift. The plane banked to the right and started to circle, its huge wings lazily sliding along the milky sky. Surely the pilot had seen him. Jon wept. The jet made a bigger circle around him, but also moved away. Thirty minutes went by. Could they see him? The plane floated back into view like a giant cruising bird. It dropped a flare. He was found.

Aboard the P-3C Orion, the crew was jubilant. Although they had marked the position and circled back, it took them several passes to relocate Jon after Gary's initial sighting. "Are you sure, are you sure?" the others asked him.

He was positive. And now they all saw it, unmistakably. The kayak, the yellow rain jacket, and Jon waving, alert and active. They dropped the flare. Jon paddled to it, hoping for food or water. There was nothing, but it hardly mattered. He would be rescued.

The navy signaled the Coast Guard with the good news. When the C-130 arrived, Gary's plane backed off to observe. Jon marveled at the two huge military planes flying figure eights above him. A yellow raft dropped through the sky, inflating on its way to the water. Jon raced to it and clambered in. He found plastic packets of water and gulped one down. The liquid slid down his parched throat, like life itself pouring back into his body.

At Barbers Point, where the Coast Guard aircraft and their crews were based, the alarm bell sounded, followed by the announcement "Missing kayaker found." Petty Officer 2nd Class Scott Gordon, a thirty-one-year-old rescue swimmer, jumped into action. He scrambled into his wet suit, grabbed his mask and fins, and raced to join his colleagues heading to the helicopter. They quickly lifted off and choppered to the southwest, past Maui, Molokaʻi, Kahoʻolawe, and Lānaʻi, then on to the Big Island. Not knowing what to expect, the crew learned enroute that Jon was still alive. This was exciting news. Scott had seen his share of false alarms as well as searches that recovered only dead bodies.

When they choppered into view, Jon was sitting in the raft, the two aircraft hovering overhead. He looked pretty good, Scott thought. Scott, however, knew that people sometimes were fueled by adrenaline at the time of rescue, only to lapse into shock soon afterward. He quickly prepared to go down and assess the situation. He strapped a harness over his wetsuit and tethered himself to a cable that dropped him through the sky. In the water, he unhooked himself and swam to the raft. He squinted up at Jon.

"How you doing?"

A smile lit the kayaker's sunburned face.

"Boy, am I glad to see you."

Scott helped Jon into a metal basket that was lowered from the helicopter and signaled his colleagues to hoist it back up. It was a textbook rescue, and soon they were choppering to Kona. Scott checked Jon's vital signs and found them surprisingly strong, although his arms and shoulders were raw, even oozing a bit, and his face had second-degree burns. Scott rubbed salve on the wounds, but was amazed at how well the hardy young man had fared.

The phone rang in Justin Acosta's home. It was his day off and he had watched the news first thing that morning only to learn that Jon was still missing. This guy is gone, he thought sadly. It's a highway to nowhere out there. The commander at work also had called him that morning, just to get his opinion on where Jon might be and what the computer was showing. The search had spread over 4,500 square miles. Justin didn't care what the computer said; he still felt Jon was moving southwest. Now it was midday and the phone was ringing again. It was the command center. Jon had been found, 120 miles southwest of the Big Island. Alive. Justin smiled.

Jon was evaluated at the hospital and reunited with his mother and two brothers, who flew in from the mainland. He got reacquainted with the use of his weakened legs. After doctors elevated his fluid levels, he left the hospital late that night, twenty-one pounds lighter for his ordeal but otherwise intact. He was a media sensation. But there would be plenty of time in the future to talk about his miracle, the divine intervention that he firmly believed had connected his phone calls. For now, he and his family checked into a hotel. He slept.

Jon Stockton made a point of meeting and thanking Justin and his other rescuers before he left the islands. He returned to Phoenix to teach in a Christian high school and continue his church work. Justin Acosta and Scott Gordon continued search-and-rescue work in the Coast Guard; Gary Phillips, flying for the navy.

Jon Stockton, 2003. Photo courtesy Jon Stockton.

References

American Lifeguard Magazine. www.usla.org/LGtoLG/Hawaii.shtml

Center for Oral History Social Science Research Institute, University of Hawai'i at Mānoa. *Tsunamis Remembered: Oral Histories of Survivors and Observers in Hawai'i.* April 2000.

CNN. "Kayaker Found in 'Miracle' Rescue." 30 July 2002.

Coleman, Stuart Holmes. *Eddie Would Go.* Honolulu: MindRaising Press, 2001.

Cox, Doak C. *Source of the Tsunami Associated with the Kalapana Earthquake of November 1975.* Honolulu: Joint Institute for Marine and Atmospheric Research, University of Hawai'i/Pacific Marine Environmental Laboratory, December 1980.

Cross, John. Personal collection. Reminiscences of Halapē survivors, November 1975.

Department of Geography, University of Hawai'i at Hilo. *Atlas of Hawai'i.* Honolulu: University of Hawai'i Press, 1998.

Department of Geography, University of Hawai'i at Mānoa. *Atlas of Hawai'i.* Honolulu: University of Hawai'i Press, 1973, 1983.

Dudley, Walter, and Min Lee. *Tsunami!* Honolulu: University of Hawai'i Press, 1998.

Fernandez, Marsue McGinnis. "Carried to Sea by a Tidal Wave." *Reader's Digest*, March 1959.

Fredericks, Anthony D. *Tsunami Man.* Honolulu: University of Hawai'i Press, 2002.

Grant, Glen, Bennett Hymer, and the Bishop Museum Archives. *Hawai'i Looking Back.* Honolulu: Mutual Publishing, 2000.

Hartwell, Jay. *Hawaiian People Today: Nā Mamo.* Honolulu: 'Ai Pōhaku Press, 1996.

Hazlett, Richard W., and Donald W. Hyndman. *Roadside Geology of Hawaii.* Missoula, Montana: Mountain Press Publishing Company, 1996.

Hawaii Tribune-Herald, 30 November–2 December, 1975.

Hawaii Tribune-Herald, 8–14 August 1976.

Hawaii Tribune-Herald, 27 November–3 December 1977.

Hawaii Tribune-Herald, 1 April 1979.

Hawaii Tribune-Herald, 1 April 1996.

Hawaii Tribune-Herald, 29 November 2000.

Hilo Tribune Herald, 2–3 April, 1946.

Honolulu Advertiser, 21 May 1961.

Honolulu Advertiser, 9–10 January 1967.

Honolulu Advertiser, 12 June 1967.

Honolulu Advertiser, 30 November–1 December 1975.

Honolulu Advertiser, 5–6 June 1979.

Honolulu Advertiser, 27 January 1992.

Honolulu Advertiser, 26 January 1993.

Honolulu Advertiser, 22 November 1994.

Honolulu Advertiser, 9–10 January 1997.

Honolulu Advertiser, 29 November 2000.

Honolulu Advertiser, 1 August 2002.

Honolulu Star-Bulletin, 6 December 1965.

Honolulu Star-Bulletin, 9 January 1967.

Honolulu Star-Bulletin, 13 March 1978.

Honolulu Star-Bulletin, 7–8 January 1997.

Honolulu Star-Bulletin, 29–30 October 1997.

Honolulu Star-Bulletin, 3 November 1997.

Honolulu Star-Bulletin, 28 October 1998.

Honolulu Star-Bulletin, 26 March 2002.

Honolulu Star-Bulletin, 31 July 2002.

Honolulu Star-Bulletin, 3 August 2002.

Honolulu Star-Bulletin, 8 September 2002.

Honolulu Star-Bulletin, 31 March 2003.

Kanayama, Richard. "Lifeguards Rescue Man from Sea-Cave." *Resources,* March 1993.

Laupāhoehoe School. *April Fool's . . . The Laupāhoehoe Tragedy of 1946, An Oral History.* Hawai'i: Laupāhoehoe School, 1997.

Laycock, George. "The Hawaiian Islands of Birds." *Audubon,* January 1970.

Los Angeles Times, 1 December 1975.

Maragos, J., and D. Gulko, eds. *Coral Reef Ecosystems of the Northwestern Hawaiian Islands: Interim Results Emphasizing the 2000 Surveys.* Honolulu: U.S. Fish and Wildlife Service and the Hawai'i Department of Land and Natural Resources.

Moi Hole rescue. Eyewitness video provided by Ralph Goto. *Navy News Online,* 9 August 2002.

NBC Dateline. Hugh Alexander story. 26 August 1998.

Simon, Scott. National Public Radio. "Surf's Up." *Weekly Edition,* 19 September 1998.

Taylor, Leighton R. *Sharks of Hawai'i: Their Biological and Cultural Significance.* Honolulu: University of Hawai'i Press, 1993.

Tsunami Museum, Hilo, Hawai'i. Displays, videos, videotaped interviews, charts and summaries related to the 1946 and 1975 tsunamis.

"Two True Stories of Scouts in Action." *Boy's Life,* March 1977.

United Press International, 31 July 2002.

U.S. Coast Guard. Jonathan Stockton rescue video, 30 July 2002.

U.S. Coast Guard. Press releases, 6 January 1997, 29–30 July 2002.

U.S. Fish and Wildlife Service, Department of the Interior. *Hawaiian Islands National Wildlife Refuge.* April 1970.

U.S. Fish and Wildlife Service, Department of the Interior. *Hawaii's Endangered Wildlife.* December 1968.

U.S. Geological Survey, Hawaiian Volcano Observatory website. "Tsunami Generated by Magnitude 7.2 Earthquake on November 29, 1975." www.usgs.gov, Volcano information.

Walker, Daniel. *Tsunami Facts*. Honolulu: School of Ocean and Earth Science and Technology, University of Hawai'i, March 1994.

West Hawaii Today, 5 August 2002.

Wright, Thomas L., Taeko Jane Takahashi, and J. D. Griggs. *Hawai'i Volcano Watch*. Honolulu: University of Hawai'i Press and Hawai'i Natural History Association, 1992.

About the Author

Rita Beamish is a veteran journalist and former White House reporter for the Associated Press. After logging many years with the AP in Los Angeles and Washington, D.C., she began her freelance career in New York, where she also taught at the Columbia University Graduate School of Journalism, before moving to Hawai'i with her husband and two daughters. Her freelance work has appeared in the *New York Times*, the *Washington Post*, *Smithsonian* magazine, *U.S. News and World Report,* and other publications.

A native of northern California, she received her B.A. degree from Santa Clara University and master's degree from the Columbia University Graduate School of Journalism. She has trekked in mountains throughout the world and enjoys Hawai'i's vast outdoor adventure opportunities.